# THE MANAGEN

## tecl

## Sultan Kermally

THOROGOOD

THE PUBLISHING BUSINESS
OF THE HAWKSMERE GROUP

**Published by Thorogood Limited**
**12-18 Grosvenor Gardens**
**London SW1W 0DH.**

**Thorogood Limited is part of the**
**Hawksmere Group of Companies.**

**www.hawksmere.co.uk**

A CIP catalogue record for this book is available from the British Library.

ISBN 1 85418 172 6 (trade edition)

ISBN 1 85418 108 4

Printed in Great Britain by Ashford Colour Press.

Designed and typeset by Paul Wallis at Thorogood.

# Contents

**CHAPTER 9NINE**
**MANAGING MEETINGS**

**CHAPTER 10TEN**
**MANAGING TIME EFFECTIVELY**

**CHAPTER 11ELEVEN**
**MANAGING PEOPLE**

## CHAPTER 14 FOURTEEN
## RE-ENGINEERING YOUR BUSINESS PROCESS

## CHAPTER 15 FIFTEEN
## MANAGING STRESS

## CHAPTER 16 SIXTEEN
## CORPORATE CULTURE

## CHAPTER 17 SEVENTEEN
## 'OUTSIDE THE BOX' THINKING

## READING TOOL BOX
## FOR BUSY MANAGERS

# The author

**Sultan Kermally**, MA., B.Sc.(Soc.), LL.B. Ph.D., Dip. Fin. and Accts., Dip. Marketing, Certificate in Further Education.

Sultan Kermally is an independent management development consultant and trainer designing and delivering training courses in Business Strategy, Business Economics, Marketing, Managing People, Performance and Knowledge and Personal Development. He has conducted training in the UK, the Netherlands, Belgium, France, Austria, the Middle East, Hong Kong and Tajikistan.

He has held senior academic positions in Scotland and thereafter senior management positions with The Management Centre Europe in Brussels, The London Business School and The Economist Intelligence Unit where he held the position of Senior Vice President of The Economist Conferences, Europe.

He has been involved in management education and development for a number of years including distance learning management education courses. He has been tutoring with the Open University and Open University Business School since their inception. Currently he is teaching the 'Performance Management and Evaluation' MBA module for the Open University Business School and 'Organisational Behaviour' MBA module for the Durham University Business School.

Sultan Kermally is the author of *Total Management Thinking*, *Management Ideas*, and *Managing Performance* and *Economics Means Business – New Economics of Information Age*.

# Introduction

Managers these days have to possess a multitude of skills in order to manage their businesses, their regions, their departments and their teams in a fast moving world. For many businesses **the future is happening now**. Managers have to plan, to organise, to co-ordinate, to communicate and to lead. This has always been the case. What has changed is the speed with which these functions have to be performed effectively.

The competitive climate is becoming very intensive. Organisations, for profit as well as 'not-for-profit', have to adapt to the changing external climate. The pace of change means managers have to make key decisions very quickly. All managers, new and experienced, have to be on a 'fast track' in order to manage effectively.

There are a variety of frameworks and tools which enable managers to make key decisions within structured frameworks. **This book is an attempt to bring most frameworks and tools together, in order to help managers perform their functions effectively**.

> **Tool boxes** provide guidance on making decisions and *Analysis tools* provide a framework to structure your thinking.

## Plan of the book

This book is divided into the following seventeen chapters.

### 1. Making decisions about strategy

This section covers the mission statement – strategic objectives – conducting environmental analysis – conducting industry analysis – conducting S.W.O.T.

## 2. Strategy evaluation

Value chain analysis – mergers and acquisitions – outsourcing – formulating and implementing strategy.

## 3. Benchmarking

This section covers the role and the nature of benchmarking and is a guide to benchmarking.

## 4. Marketing

Market research – concept of goods and services – customer service – understanding your markets – segmentation – customer base – marketing strategy – positioning – marketing mix – pricing – brands – market planning.

## 5. Total Quality Management

Basic tools – quality awards – the European quality management – ISO 9000 – quality management system – environmental management system.

## 6. Finance

Calculating financial ratios – interpreting financial ratios – making break-even decisions – making sense of financial statements.

## 7. Making decisions

Decision styles – making structured decisions.

## 8. Managing performance

Balanced scorecard approach.

## 9. Managing meetings

Reasons for holding meetings. Role of a chairman – preparation.

## 10. Managing your time

Meaning of time – your personal and professional goals – prioritising your needs – steps to behavioural change.

## 11. Managing people

Leadership – motivation – recruitment – interviewing – delegation – empowerment – staff performance – coaching – building teams.

## 12. Communication

Assessing your communication effectiveness. Negotiating your way to success. Communicating assertively.

## 13. Managing change

Techniques used. Deciding on enablers and resistors.

## 14. Business process re-engineering

What it is and how to re-engineer your business processes.

## 15. Managing stress

Pressure v. stress – causes and symptoms.

## 16. Corporate culture

What is culture? – role of culture.

## 17. 'Outside the box' thinking

Breaking out of your perceptions – unlearning.

# CHAPTER 1ONE

# Strategy

# Strategy

**FORMULATING BUSINESS STRATEGY** involves making decisions on business direction, assessing sources of competitive advantage, examining external factors, taking into consideration aspirations and interests of all stakeholders, conducting organisational audit and then deciding on people, processes and products in order to gain and sustain competitive advantage. This chapter deals with appropriate **tool boxes** to structure your thinking and action to formulate an appropriate business strategy.

Every business requires a direction. This direction is influenced by an organisation's mission. An organisation needs to have mission in order to articulate its corporate vision. Mission is about an organisation's philosophy of how it intends to conduct itself.

---

### TOOL BOX 1ONE

**What should a mission statement contain?**

In preparing a mission statement ask yourself these questions:

1. What does your organisation stand for?
2. What does it believe in?
3. What does it expect from its employees in terms of their behaviour?

---

Mission statements should be focused and should be easy to understand in terms of behaviours and standards.

After preparing a mission the next step is to prepare strategy for the organisation. *Strategy provides the direction and goals.* According to Michael Porter, strategy is a combination of the goals for which the organisation is striving and the means by which it is seeking to get there. To focus on a meaningful direction and prepare appropriate strategy, top management have to consider asking and answering the following questions:

---

**TOOL BOX 2TWO**

**Deciding on business direction**

**A.** What business are we In?

**B.** What do we want to achieve?

**C.** How are we going to achieve them?

**D.** What is the timescale involved?

---

Answering the above questions will give direction to your business and clarify your business objectives and the time within which you want to achieve your objectives.

The four questions in **Tool box 2** appear very simple but they are fundamental questions all businesses should address to provide a clear strategy. For example, if you are in the business of making ice cream, in addressing a question 'What business are we in?' you ask yourself are we making a product which is called and recognised as ice cream or are we making a product which is not just going to meet the demand but create delight and excitement for consumers? If this is the case then you are in the business of making ice cream that would thrill and excite consumers. This will affect your decision to make a product with different colours, different flavours and different attributes (softness, texture etc).

Having answered the questions in **Tool box 2** you then proceed to formulate your business or strategic objectives. Objectives could be financial such as gross profit margin or net margin or profit per employee or cost of sales etc or non-financial such as satisfying customers, providing a very high quality product or increasing the volume of repeat business etc. In practice, strategic objectives are financial and non-financial. It is very important when formulating objectives to consider the criteria in **Toolbox 3**. If these criteria are ignored, there will be considerable frustrations in assessing business results.

### TOOL BOX 3THREE

#### Criteria for setting strategic objectives

**S**  Objectives should be simple and sensible and stretched to deploy fully the resources available. They should make sense to all those involved in achieving them.

**M**  Objectives should be measurable. It is said that what gets measured gets done.

**A**  They should be attainable and not be far-fetched.

**R**  They should be realistic.

**T**  They should have a timescale. Achievement should be measured within the context of different timescales. They could be every three months or six months or three years, whatever makes sense to the business.

Once the strategic objectives have passed the S.M.A.R.T. criteria highlighted in Toolbox 3, it is important to then consider the interests and aspirations of stakeholders. Stakeholders are groups of people who have direct interests in the performance of your business. The stakeholder groups are investors, managers, employees, customers, suppliers and, in some cases, regulators and the government departments.

## Levels of strategy

The questions in **Tool box 1** and **2** relate to corporate level strategy. The tactics of achieving corporate strategy lead to formulation of strategy at business unit level. How is an organisation going to achieve its strategic objectives? Second level or business level strategy focuses on how business units within the organisation are going to achieve these objectives. Business level strategies and objectives must be consistent with corporate level strategies.

# Why is strategy important?

*'All men can see the tactics whereby I conquer but what none see is the strategy out of which great victory is evolved.'*

**SUN TZU**
Chinese military strategist (3000 years ago).

The business environment is changing dramatically and in a such a world, strategy also has to be dynamic. There is a need to adapt strategy according to the changes in the business environment within which business is operating. This is known as strategic adaptation. To bring about such a 'fit' between corporate strategy and an external environment it is important to undertake environmental analysis.

Changes in environmental factors can be categorised into sociological factors (S), technological factors (T), economic factors (E), and political factors (P). These S.T.E.P. factors have impact on business performance.

**Sociological factors** incorporate changes in social attitude (attitude towards smoking or drug taking for example), changes in social habits and behaviour, ageing population, more women working etc.

**Technological factors** include technological developments in relation to computing, teleworking, faxes, telecommunications, etc.

**Economic factors** relate to inflation, employment, economic growth, exchange and interest rates for example.

**Political factors** relate to policies of deregulation, privatisation, free trade etc.

It is very important for any organisation to undertake analysis of how such factors affect their business. Based on this analysis the organisation can then adjust its strategy.

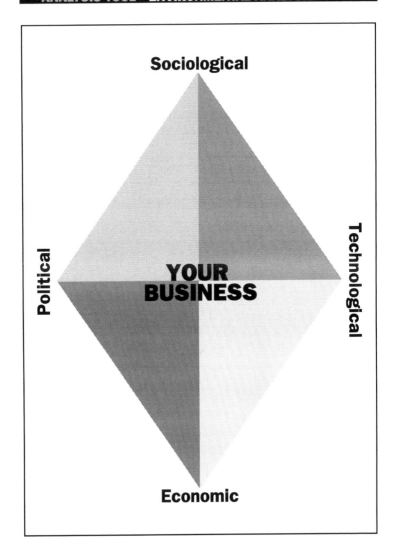

## Conducting environmental analysis

*Step one*

Consider all key factors under S.T.E.P. categories (see p.11) and identify those factors which affect your business directly. For example, interest rates under economic factors affect building trade directly or the ageing population impacts on financial services industries.

*Step two*

Having gathered all the factors that have relevance to your business, consider the probability of change in relation to these factors. For example, how probable it is for exchange rates to change in the near future. The scale of probability should be 'high' and 'low'. (**See Toolbox 5**).

*Step three*

Consider the impact of these factors. Should the probability of change and impact on business put all these factors in box 'A' in **Toolbox 5**.

*Step four*

In the light of this information, should your strategy and associated strategic objectives be revised, fine-tuned or reformulated?

## TOOL BOX 5FIVE

### Conducting impact analysis of S.T.E.P. factors

**Probability of change**

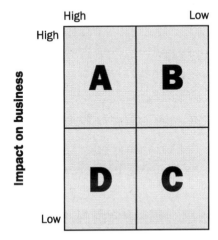

Under each heading of sociological, technological, economic and political factors identify key elements (for example, interest rates, Britain joining the single currency, new technology etc) and assess its probability of change and its subsequent impact on your business. If probability of change is **high** and its impact on your business is **high** it would fall in box A.

Consider all the items that fall in 'A' before formulating your strategy.

Having completed an analysis of external factors, the next step is to analyse the industry within which your business operates. This is known as undertaking industry analysis. Michael Porter presented a five forces framework to undertake industry analysis. These are:

rivalry among competitors, bargaining power of suppliers, bargaining power of buyers, substitutes and barriers to entry.

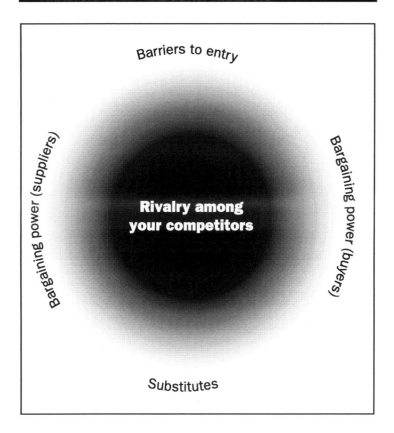

- What kind of competition exists?
- What is the intensity of competition?
- How strong is the bargaining power of suppliers and buyers?
- What are the barriers to entering your market?
- What substitutes exist in relation to your product and service?

### Conducting industry analysis

The following factors should be taken into account when conducting industry analysis.

- How many firms/organisations are there in the industry you are operating?
- What is the relative size of their business?
- What is their market share?
- How fast are they growing?
- What is their cost structure?
- What is their profitability?
- What kind of distribution channels do they deal with?
- How much do they spend on research and product development?
- What is their advertising/promotion policy?
- What type of resources do they have?

Industry analysis will provide an organisation with useful information about the competitive environment and its business rivals.

Having accumulated information on external and industry factors, an organisation then has to conduct an audit of its current capabilities and the challenges that lie ahead. The method for doing that is known as undertaking a **S.W.O.T. analysis**. This analysis involves examining the Strengths, Weaknesses, Opportunities and Threats facing an organisation.

## TOOL BOX 7SEVEN

### Conducting S.W.O.T. analysis

*Strengths*
Looking inside your organisation, what strengths do you have in relation to your strategy, structure, people, leadership, processes, products, systems, values, culture?

*Weaknesses*
What weaknesses do you have in relation to the above factors?

*Opportunities*
In scanning the external environment and having undertaken industry analysis, what opportunities do you see for your business? Make a list of these opportunities.

*Threats*
In looking externally, what challenges do you face? Make a list.

### ANALYSIS TOOL • S.W.O.T

| | | |
|---|---|---|
| Strengths | Weaknesses | External perspective |
| Opportunities | Threats | Internal perspective |

Please note that **strengths and weaknesses** relate to factors **inside** your organisation, whereas **threats and opportunities** relate to factors **outside** your organisation.

*Gaining competitive advantage involves analysing internal and external sources.*

Michael Porter has highlighted two basic types of competitive advantage. They are competitive advantage focusing on **cost leadership** and the other type focusing on **differentiation**. Whether you go for competitive cost advantage or differentiation depends on the resources you have available, what competencies your organisation possesses in terms of processes and people, your competitive environment, the nature of your business and your business strategy.

Having undertaking various analyses you then have to proceed to formulate your business strategy and strategic objectives. Objectives are expressed in quantitative terms for example, achieving 15 per cent net margin by the end of the budget period or reducing overhead costs by 25 per cent over the next three years or qualitative terms, for example, meeting customer needs or producing quality products.

# CHAPTER 2TWO

## Strategy evaluation

# Strategy evaluation

**STRATEGY NEEDS TO** be evaluated. The criteria of evaluation are as follows:

The main rationale behind corporate strategy is to gain and sustain competitive advantage in the area you want to do business in. This is why it is very important at very outset to ask a question 'What business are we in?'.

Michael Porter presented the concept of '**value chain**' which incorporates discrete activities that lead to satisfying customer needs. These activities relate to production, sales, finance, human relations procurement, technology and service. All these activities are interrelated.

Porter suggested focusing attention on a value chain to create and sustain competitive advantage. Activities that do not add value serve no purpose in achieving strategic objectives.

---

**TOOL BOX 9NINE**

**Analysis of value chain**

1. Identify all activities involved in different processes. For example, processes involved in production or selling or managing people.
2. Ask a simple question. Within each process which activities add value to customer satisfaction?
3. Eliminate activities that do not add value to a given process.

---

Elimination of such activities will release some resources and strengthen the organisation's capability to compete.

Strategic objectives, once formulated, should be communicated to all regions, departments, divisions and teams. It is important that departmental or regional or divisional strategies should be consistent with overall corporate strategies.

Strategic objectives should be measured and monitored. In implementing strategy, objectives should be monitored regularly (every three months for example) and should be fine-tuned or adjusted to fit the changing business environment. There should be a **strategic fit** between the organisation and the environment within which it operates.

This is known as '**control loop**'. See overleaf.

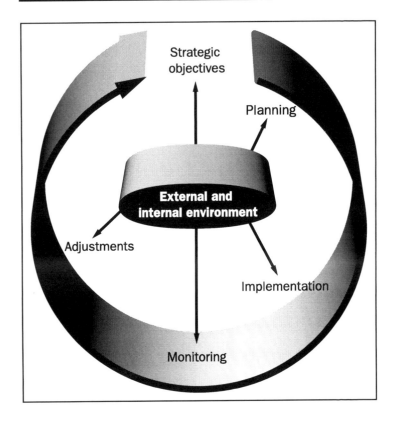

The main objectives behind measuring strategic objectives are to survive and grow and if you are a commercial organisation to make profit.

In terms of growth and survival, an organisation has various options known as **strategic options**. It can decide to grow internally by using its available resources (this is known as growing organically) or it can decide to grow by acquiring other organisations or making alliances with other organisations (growth by acquisitions and alliances).

Growing organically takes time because an organisation has to develop its capabilities and create new competencies. Some organisations prefer to grow organically in order to avoid a clash of cultures or to develop their capabilities and competencies to tailor their business aspirations.

## Why acquire companies?

- To improve competitive positioning vis-à-vis its rivals.

- To acquire new competencies very quickly.

- To gain market share.

- To gain effective distribution channel.

- To achieve economies of scale.

- To become a key global player.

- To respond to the growth strategy of its competitors.

- To collaborate on research and development.

- To overcome local market peculiarities.

- To gain new knowledge.

- To create and achieve synergy.

**Before acquiring any company ask the following questions:**

---

**TOOL BOX 10TEN**

## To merge or not to merge?

- Why do I want to acquire?
- Can I achieve my objectives by developing resources and competencies internally?
- Have I done appropriate and adequate research on market potential?
- Does merger fit my strategic objectives?
- What plan do I have for integrating two businesses?
- What plan do I have to assimilate different organisational cultures?
- Are there any dangers for personality clashes at top management level?
- Have I properly estimated the potential for synergy?
- How is the merged company going to be organised?
- Is there a strategic fit?
- What systems am I going to put in place to make a merger succeed?

---

There are various strategic options undertaken by companies in practice. Instead of merging, some businesses form alliances. Alliances can be formed with competitors, or with complementors or with suppliers, distributors and so on. The reasons behind alliances could be to share research and development cost, to share expensive technology or specialised knowledge, to improve marketing effectiveness and so on. In some cases one of the strategic options adopted is to outsource certain functions or activities in order to reduce costs or to improve the effectiveness of certain processes or activities within the value chain.

Some organisations outsource their IT function, some their accounting function or human resources function or logistics. Outsourcing is simply the transfer of a specific activity or process or function to a different organisation so that the organisation can focus its attention and deploy resources to focus on core activities. The outside organisation thus takes the responsibility of managing that specific function to meet your organisational needs.

Before you decide to outsource any function, consider the following:

---

**TOOL BOX 11 ELEVEN**

**Outsourcing – your place or mine?**

1. Why do you want to outsource?
2. What is it you want to outsource?
3. Who are you outsourcing to and why?
4. What guarantees do you have of quality of service?
5. Have you asked for references?
6. What kind of a deal you want to make?
7. How long is the deal for?
8. Do you have an escape clause without incurring a penalty?
9. Who on your side is going to manage the relationship?
10. Why have you chosen that particular person?

---

Outsourcing has now become an important way of enabling organisations to remain responsive to market needs. Outsourcing is not taken for purely 'outloading' reasons. Companies now make outsourcing decisions on a strategic basis. Few companies can cope with increasing costs of keeping up with large number of different technologies. Outsourcing of any function or operation should be part of an overall strategic framework that takes into account corporate objectives.

---

**TOOL BOX 12TWELVE**

**The key stages of formulating and implementing business strategy**

1. Prepare a mission statement.
2. Formulate your company strategy.
3. Prepare strategic objectives.
4. Devise strategic performance measures.
5. Implement your strategy.
6. Measure performance indicators and compare against your strategic objectives.
7. Correct deviances and make adjustments.

---

# Strategic performance

Once you have formulated your strategy and strategic objectives, you then have to have strategic measures to monitor your business performance. Strategic measures could be financial, such as return on capital employed, gross or net margin, profit per project or per employee or the measures could be non-financial such as delivery time, response rate or staff turnover rate. Whether these measures are financial or non-financial, quantitative or qualitative, these measures must be monitored to see if the business is on the right track.

Being on the right track is not enough these days. You have to move fast otherwise you will be taken over or run over.

Many businesses now track their competitors and benchmark against ' best practice' performers in order to compete effectively. The practice of benchmarking is becoming increasingly popular.

# CHAPTER 3THREE

# Benchmarking for best practice

# Benchmarking for best practice

**BENCHMARKING IS A** method of improving business performance by learning from other companies or departments how to do things better in order to be the 'best in class'.

To undertake benchmarking you have to be very systematic and the whole process should be continuous and should involve evaluation and measurement.

Benchmarking can only happen in a culture in which people are prepared to have their thinking challenged and are prepared to learn from one another.

Benchmarking offers the following advantages:

- Provides direction and impetus for improvement.
- Gives early warning of competitive disadvantage.
- Promotes competitive awareness.
- Leads to stepping stones to breakthrough thinking.
- Identifies the 'best practice'.
- Provides an objective attainment standard for key areas of business operations.
- Links operational tactics to corporate vision and strategy.
- Identifies performance gaps.
- Triggers major step change in business performance.
- Helps companies redefine their corporate objectives.

## TOOL BOX 13THIRTEEN

### Benchmarking think-tank

1. Why do you want to benchmark?
2. What is it you want to benchmark?
3. What specific outcomes are you expecting?
4. Are there best performers within the organisation or outside the organisation?
5. What type of organisation would you like to benchmark against and why?
6. What information would you need to get from a comparator organisation?
7. Where would you find this information?
8. Who should you involve in a benchmarking team and why?
9. How should you start the process and who should do it?
10. How do you communicate information?
11. Once we get the information, what do you do with it?
12. How do you bring about the change?
13. Who should be responsible for constantly monitoring the change?
14. How do you propose to communicate the results throughout the organisation?

Once you have answered all the questions satisfactorily you are then ready to proceed to benchmark.

### How to benchmark

1. Identify the company or department or process or function you want to benchmark.

2. Identify the best practice.

3. Start collecting information.

4. Analyse this information and determine the gaps that exist in your practice.

5. Start formulating project proposal and determine on outcomes.

6. Communicate gaps as well as project objectives to all those to be involved.

7. Initiate change and communicate results.

8. Develop action plan.

9. Appoint project leader or co-ordinator.

10. Implement action plan and monitor results.

There are different types of benchmarking:

**Competitive bench-marking** involves seeking information from and of competitors to determine best practice. **Strategic benchmarking** involves developing measures for a business which quantify its key strengths and weaknesses to give some external reference to the strategic planning process. **Process benchmarking** involves comparing internal processes between companies, countries or divisions within the same group. **Product benchmarking** involves comparing products of competitors in relation to, for example, functionality, reliability and availability. **Functional benchmarking** involves comparisons of specific functions such as finance, marketing, human resources with a view to enhancing functional effectiveness. **Internal benchmarking** is undertaken within the organisation or within the same group of companies.

---

**TOOL BOX 15FIFTEEN**

### Where to get the information to benchmark?

Some of the sources of information are:

▶ Annual reports.

▶ Press information.

▶ Consultants' or analysts' reports.

▶ Market research reports.

▶ Trade associations.

▶ Academic case studies.

▶ Conferences and seminars.

▶ Benchmarking clubs.

▶ Joint-venture partners.

▶ Site visits.

▶ Consumer surveys.

▶ Retail audits.

▶ Salesmen.

▶ Product comparisons.

▶ Distributors and suppliers.

---

▲ ▲ ▲ ▲ ▲ ▲ ▲ ▲ ▲ ▲ ▲ ▲ ▲ ▲

# CHAPTER 4FOUR

# Marketing

# Marketing

**MARKETING IS IMPORTANT** for all businesses, big or small, for profit and not-for-profit. Peter Drucker emphasised the importance of marketing by saying that marketing is business and business is all about marketing. Marketing is defined as anticipation and satisfaction of demand through the exchange process. Businesses produce goods and provide services in order to satisfy consumers' needs.

How can a business anticipate and subsequently satisfy consumers' needs? This is done by market research.

**What is market research?** It is a systematic method of gathering information and analysing information relating to marketing your goods and services. It can be undertaken by businesses themselves or by outside agencies and consultancies.

**TOOL BOX 16 SIXTEEN**

### How to undertake market research

1. Decide what information you want to get. This will be determined by the decision you are faced with. If you know what problem you are faced with, then this will help you get targeted information.

2. Why do you want this information? The answer will focus your attention on a problem you want to solve.

3. How are you going to get this information? Are you going to use internal or external resources?

4. If you are going to use internal resources, can you afford to do so? Will the deployment of these resources have any knock-on effect on existing activities and functions, and, if so, what provisions are you going to make?

5. If you are going to use external resources, can you afford them? Are you in a position to give them a precise brief in relation to the information you require and why you require it?

6. Set a time limit of gathering research.

7. How are you going to handle information? Again, will this information be analysed internally or externally?

8. Internally, have you got the resources and expertise within the organisation?

9. Has the analysis generated results to enable you to solve your initial problem?

10. How do you propose to implement the results?

11. How are you going to monitor implementation?

Gathering information about your market is very important. If you are starting a new business then you want to know if there is a market for your product or service. In fact, in raising finance for your business, the financing agency would expect you to provide information on the market you want to enter. If you are already in a business then you can do market research. When you launch a new product or service, or if you want to find out if your market is changing and how you could respond to your customers' needs. The main objective of the market research is to find out **what you can sell rather than to sell what you can make**.

# The concept of goods and services

To satisfy consumers' demand and expectations you will need to consider the nature of the product you produce or the nature of the service you provide. You have to pay special attention to quality, performance and function.

Consumers buy services and products if they consider they are getting value from their purchase. They estimate value in relation to the benefits they derive from their purchase. For marketing to be effective, producers have to **sell benefits** rather than product or service attributes.

When people buy products or services they expect to meet their expectations in terms of reliability, performance, durability, certainty, comfort, image and so on. Customer's perception of the product/ service determines the success for business. It is said that 'what customers perceive, customers should receive'.

Many businesses are now transforming themselves to become customer-driven organisations. DHL, Fed Express, British Telecom, ABB, AT&T, Rank Xerox ICL, and many other companies have realised that it is not *what* you make but it is *how* you meet total satisfaction and how you deliver and treat your customers that enable organisations to sustain their competitive advantage.

In order to provide service quality, organisations have to aim at being in box A in the diagram opposite.

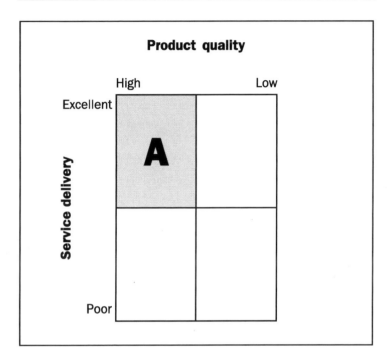

**Delivering service excellence is the norm for many businesses nowadays.**

## Providing a good customer service

Many organisations install very expensive systems to improve their customer service. In spite of massive investment they cannot understand how they still lose customers. To provide good customer service it is important to have employees who have consideration and care for the customers. If employees are not properly trained and if they are unhappy in the organisations they work for, then there will be very poor customer service or if there is good customer service then it will be very temporary.

Organisations first have to care for their employees and give them the opportunity to feel 'I'm OK'. They should then train their employees to have high consideration for their customers and create 'You're OK' feeling. See previous page, 'Delivering service quality.' To sustain competitive advantage and sustain good customer service, efforts should be made to position employees in box A.

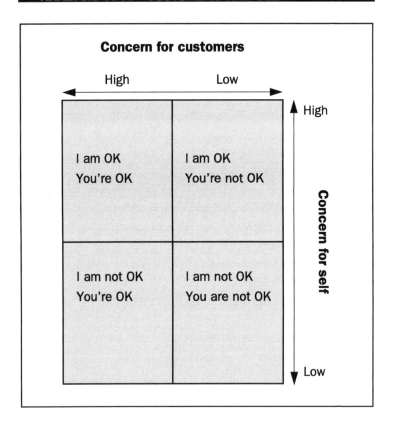

To provide good customer service should be the objective of every person in the organisation.

## How to create good customer service

1. Do not pay lip service to customer service.

2. Do not create policies to exclude customers' needs. (Do not say 'I am sorry but it is not our policy...')

3. Do have conviction and commitment in providing good customer service.

4. Make customer satisfaction the core of your corporate strategy.

5. Top and senior managers should not remain remote from customers.

6. Visit and talk to your customers regularly and listen to their demands and note their needs.

7. Do not fall into a trap of thinking you provide good customer care just because you have customer service desks or departments.

8. Empower your staff to make key decisions at the coal face to solve customer problems.

9. Allocate resources to provide good customer service and train your staff.

10. Customer care is everybody's responsibility.

## Consider the following story

This is a story about four people named *Everybody*, *Somebody*, *Anybody* and *Nobody*.

There was an important job to be done to improve customer service and *Everybody* was sure that *Somebody* would do it.

*Anybody* could have done it but *Nobody* did it.

*Somebody* got angry about that because it was *Everybody's* job. *Everybody* thought *Anybody* could do it.

But *Nobody* realised that *Everybody* would not do it.

It ended up that *Everybody* blamed *Somebody* when *Nobody* did what *Anybody* could have done.

# How to find out about what customers need

The following methods are used by many organisations:

- Market research.

- Customer satisfaction surveys.

- Analysis and management of complaints.

- Analysis of lost customers to find out why they have deserted you.

- Customers' panels and advisory committees.

- Regular customer visits.

## Understanding your markets

Your markets consist of people. It is very important to understand the population size, gender and age of the market you are dealing with. These are called demographic factors and they have a bearing on how you are going to **segment your market**. If the population in a market you are dealing with is growing very slowly then you will be dealing with an ageing population. There will be a significant proportion of older people and their needs, interests and aspirations will be different from the population which is dominated by young people.

It is very important to decide which population segment you want to deal with. Do you want to deal with young people or older people?

Male or female? Ethnic or native? Professional or other workers? Married people or single parents or single people? Is there any particular social class you want to deal with? These questions have to be asked and answers arrived at before any market research is conducted or any marketing strategy is formulated.

Identifying your market segments will enable you target efficiently and effectively. Market segments are identifiable groups within a market that you propose to do business with. **Niche** is a very narrow segment with distinct needs and interests.

Please note that market segments do change over time. It is, therefore, very important to monitor the changes in the segments you are dealing in and dealing with.

There are four bases of segmenting your markets. These are as follows:

## Demographic

This relates to age, gender, family size, income, occupation, education race and religion of population in question.

## Geographic

This relates to the regions, cities, densities and climate.

## Psychographic

This refers to class structure and lifestyles of segments of the population.

## Behavioural

This refers to benefits and behavioural patterns of different segments of population.

Bases of segmentation determine the marketing mix and the way products/services are to be marketed.

## Purchasing: actual v. potential

You may undertake research on purchasing habits of your market segment but beware of actual and potential purchasing decisions. For example, if you are manufacturing cars, cleaning equipment, or medical instruments it is not enough to ascertain how many people will buy specific products. You may have $x$ number of people actually buying medical equipment but not necessarily your brand or the equipment you manufacture. It is important to get some information on total purchase and relate this information to actual sales of your products. This will give you an idea of potential market available and how you should convert this potential to actual by appropriate promotional strategy.

## Maintain your customer base

In any business it is important to monitor and maintain the customer base. Your customer base is the result of the winners and losers from particular segments. See below.

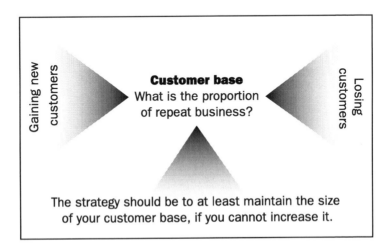

**ANALYSIS TOOL · CUSTOMER BASE**

Gaining new customers

**Customer base**
What is the proportion
of repeat business?

Losing customers

The strategy should be to at least maintain the size
of your customer base, if you cannot increase it.

Understanding and analysing your customer base will give you information on repeat business and the degree of customer loyalty your business commands.

# Marketing strategy

Marketing strategy should go hand-in-hand with business strategy. In considering the growth strategy of each business or product division the technique developed by the Boston Consulting Group could be used. This technique involves assessing market share of each business or product division and the annual rate of market growth. See below.

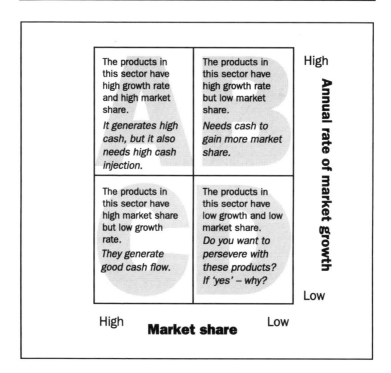

**ANALYSIS TOOL · PRODUCT STRATEGY**

The products in this sector have high growth rate and high market share.
*It generates high cash, but it also needs high cash injection.*

The products in this sector have high growth rate but low market share.
*Needs cash to gain more market share.*

High

The products in this sector have high market share but low growth rate.
*They generate good cash flow.*

The products in this sector have low growth and low market share.
*Do you want to persevere with these products? If 'yes' – why?*

Low

**Annual rate of market growth**

High    **Market share**    Low

## Product strategy

**Box A** indicates the business has a good growth rate but it has a high market share. The marketing strategy here would be to decide whether to invest in businesses falling in this sector A in order to increase relative market share.

**Box B** indicates 'stars'. The company needs to invest and come up with a marketing strategy to sustain 'star' quality.

**Box C**. Businesses have high market share and generate cash for the company. This is a 'cash cow' sector. As the market growth rate is low the company does not have to invest too much for this business.

**Box D** businesses are weak. The decision has to be made to either abandon this business or to bring about improvements.

The other technique related to marketing strategy was introduced by Igor Ansoff. (See analysis tool, opposite.)

The company can either adopt **market penetration strategy** or **market development strategy** or **product development strategy** or **diversification strategy** depending on markets and product situations.

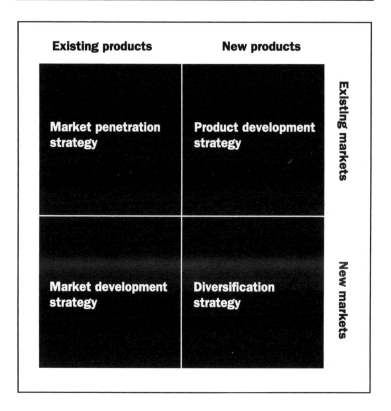

|  | **Existing products** | **New products** |  |
|---|---|---|---|
| **Existing markets** | Market penetration strategy | Product development strategy | |
| **New markets** | Market development strategy | Diversification strategy | |

Adopting appropriate marketing strategy depends on corporate objectives and the results of any S.W.O.T. and S.T.E.P. Analyses undertaken by an organisation.

## Positioning

Some businesses, like various airlines position themselves in customers' eyes as low price organisations but offer acceptable no-frill quality, and some like to be perceived as high price high quality businesses.

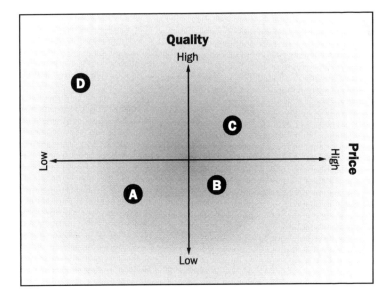

You can be at A low price – low quality business or at B high-price-low quality business or at C high-price medium-quality business or at D, low-price high-quality business. How do you want your business to be perceived?

# Marketing mix

Marketing involves the following decisions:

- What product to produce?
- What price should be charged?
- Where should products be sold?
- How should products be promoted?

These are called the **four Ps** of marketing – **Product**, **Price**, **Place** and **Promotion**.

## TOOL BOX 18EIGHTEEN

### Determining marketing mix

*Product*
- Decide on the products to be produced.
- What should be the quality?
- What features should products incorporate?
- Decide on packages including guarantees and warranties.
- How to sell these products.
- What should be the brand, if any?
- How these products should be sold/distributed/delivered.

*Price*
- What should be the list/book price?
- What discounts to offer?
- Do they compare favourably with competitors' prices?
- How does price relate to quality?
- Price and elasticity of demand?
- Credit terms available.

*Place*
- Where to find channels of distribution?
- Home market or overseas market?
- How many outlets to sell through?
- Decisions on locations.
- Logistics of distribution.

*Promotion*
- How to promote products.
- What media to use?
- What type of advertising?
- What type of sales force?
- Need for public relations.
- The image to pursue.
- Level of customer service and customer care.

Product, price, place and promotion are major components of the marketing mix that is used in different combinations depending on the nature of business and conditions of business.

In an age when businesses are becoming customer-driven, the marketing mix should be viewed from the point of consumption rather than production. Instead of thinking about 4 Ps (Product, Place, Price Promotion) of the marketing mix it should be viewed as 4 Cs – Communication, Convenience, Cost and Customer Care.

Businesses should **communicate** benefits; show how committed they are in providing good **customer care**; what is going to be the **cost** to the customer and how **convenient** the product/ service will be to them.

# A word on price elasticity

Price elasticity is a concept used in economics to refer to responsiveness of demand to price changes. Generally speaking, as price falls quantities demanded (sales) increase and as price rises quantities demanded (sales) decrease. This is known as law of demand in economics.

However, in order to sell more it is not always the case that revenue will be increased by lowering the price of products. Whether total revenue increases or decreases in response to price, variations depend on the elasticity of demand.

Price elasticity could be either **elastic** or **inelastic**. If demand of a product is elastic then within a certain price range total revenue will increase as price drops and total revenue will decrease as price increases. See 'Elastic demand' opposite, showing behaviour of a product which has elastic demand.

## Elastic demand

| Quantity Units | Price/Product £ | Total/Revenue £ |
|---|---|---|
| 10 | 10 | 100 |
| 8 | 15 | 120 |
| 6 | 25 | 150 |

If total revenue decreases due to price decrease or total revenue increases due to price increase the demand for a product is inelastic. See 'Inelastic demand' below, showing behaviour of a product which has inelastic demand.

## Inelastic demand

| Quantity Units | Price/Product £ | Total/Revenue £ |
|---|---|---|
| 10 | 10 | 100 |
| 12 | 9 | 108 |
| 15 | 8 | 120 |
| 8 | 12 | 96 |
| 6 | 14 | 84 |

It is also possible for total revenue to remain constant as price of a product changes. In this case the product has unit elasticity. See 'Unit elasticity' below, for a product which has unit elasticity.

## Unit elasticity

| Quantity | Price/Product | Total/Revenue |
|:---:|:---:|:---:|
| Units | £ | £ |
| 10 | 4 | 40 |
| 20 | 2 | 40 |
| 8 | 5 | 40 |

# Brands

A brand is a name, a symbol or design associated with particular products or services. *The Economist*, BMW, Coca Cola, Pepsi Cola, IBM, Calvin Klein, Gucci, are all examples of brand name.

According to Philip Kotler, 'a brand is a seller's promise to consistently deliver a specific set of features, benefits, and services to buyers. The best brands convey a warranty of quality.'

## Properties of brands

- Brands convey certain attributes such as quality, speed, excellence, durability, uniqueness etc.
- Brands convey benefits to customers such as usefulness, durability, status etc.
- Brands also represent buyers' values.
- Brands reinforce overall product/service concept.

Most of the brand products bear manufacturers' brands. Own label brands are available in stores such as Sainsburys and Tesco.

Brands are created to create loyalty, perceived quality and product awareness.

## Why do companies want to brand their products?

- They want to be associated with properties of brands highlighted previously.
- They want to create barrier to entry.
- They find it easier to track down orders and track problems.
- They want to convey to their customers that they do add value and should become the preferred choice.

Establishing any brand in the market involves:

**Brand positioning**: How one particular brand relates to other brands in the market.

**Brand personality**: Establishing a relationship between the brand and its users.

**Brand property**: Communicating benefits to users.

Brands have to be managed and maintained. They must live up to their claims otherwise they will soon disappear from the market.

# Market planning

Having formulated a business strategy and a marketing strategy and having decided on the marketing mix, it is now appropriate to prepare the marketing plan.

A marketing plan consists of detailed marketing strategies and programmes for achieving the objectives set for producing products or providing services in a target market.

---

**TOOL BOX 19NINETEEN**

### How to prepare a marketing plan

**Step 1:** Analyse marketing opportunities.

**Step 2:** Undertake market research to understand and select your targets.

**Step 3:** Formulate your marketing strategies.

**Step 4:** Prepare a plan of how you are going to market.

**Step 5:** Organise, manage and control marketing efforts.

---

Marketing plans should be presented in a report format incorporating the following:

- Executive summary.

- Present market conditions.

- Opportunities and challenges for your business.

- What is your marketing strategy.

- Your marketing efforts to implement your strategy.

- How you are going to measure and monitor your marketing efforts.

# CHAPTER 5FIVE

# Total quality management

# Total Quality Management

**THE 1980s SAW** many organisations taking initiatives to adopt total quality management. Total Quality Management (TQM) is about continuous improvement in business performance with a view to meeting the needs of customers. Quality gurus like Joseph Juran, W. Edwards Deming emphasised the importance of top management commitment, effective leadership and training in succeeding at TQM. Deming introduced a very simple method of problem-solving known as the Deming Cycle. See below.

**ANALYSIS TOOL • THE DEMING CYCLE**

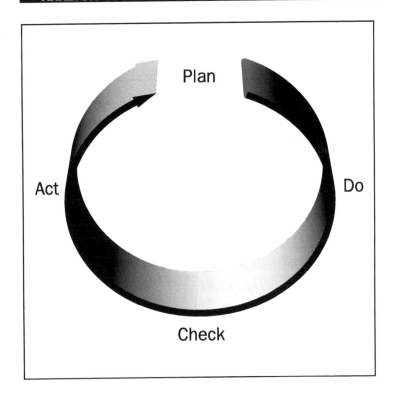

There are some basic tools which can be used in practice to monitor quality. These are very simple non-sophisticated tools. They are control charts, Pareto charts, fishbone diagrams, run charts, histograms, scatter diagrams, and flow charts.

## Control chart

Normal specifications on the vertical axis are measured and on the horizontal axis are samples of products taken to measure against specification. The chart also shows upper, lower and average tolerance limits, see below. The control chart shows whether a product is within normal specifications. Samples are selected on random basis.

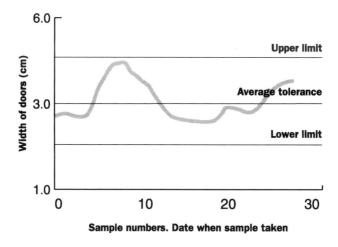

## Pareto chart

This is sometimes known as 80:20 chart. The Pareto Principle states that 80 per cent of results are caused by 20 per cent of causes. A Pareto chart is used to focus attention on 20 per cent of factors contributing to product defects.

On the vertical axis of the Pareto chart is measured the number of defects per day or week or month or whatever other appropriate time period is used. The types of defect are measured on the horizontal axis. (See below).

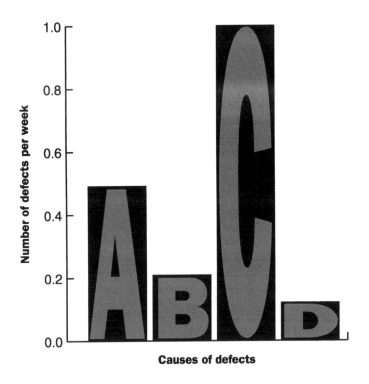

## Fishbone diagram

In this diagram the effect is shown at the end of a horizontal arrow and potential causes are shown as labelled arrows connected to the main arrow. Each of these causes may have sub-cause arrows as appropriate. This diagram focuses attention on causes and sub-causes leading to specific defect. (See below.)

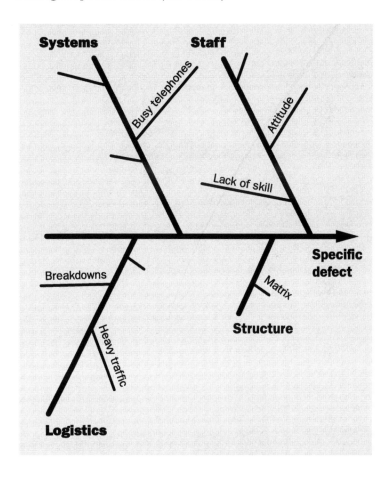

## Run charts

This chart shows a running tally of data points over a specific time reference. It is used to indicate specific times or periods (specific days or seasons, for example) when various problems are prone to occur. (See below.)

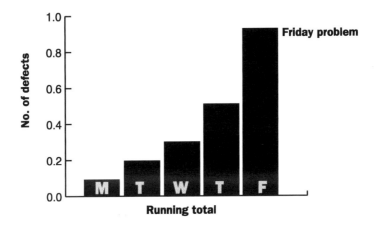

## Histograms

This is also known as a bar chart. Instead of a graph, bars are drawn next to each other to facilitate comparison of data. (See below.)

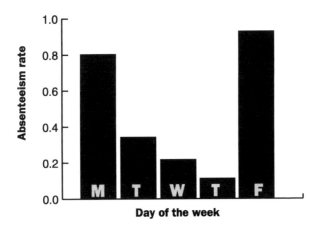

## Scatter diagram

A scatter diagram is used to establish a potential relationship between two factors, for example, speed of delivery and number of complaints. (See below).

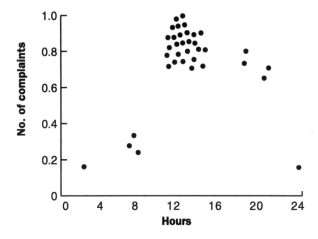

## Flow chart

This is a visual presentation of a step-by-step activity to achieve an end result. (See below.)

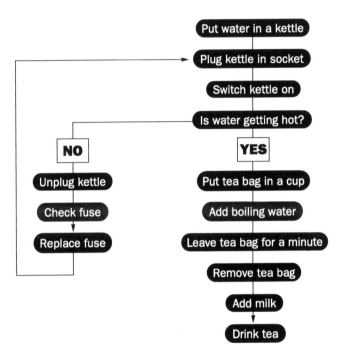

These tools are very handy to use in monitoring the quality of products or service.

# Quality awards

European quality awards are given to organisations who show excellence in the management of quality. This involves meeting the standards prescribed by the European Foundation for Quality Management. Organisations who enter for awards are assessed and scored on a scale from 0 to 1000 points as per the European Model for Total Quality Management. (See below.)

## The European quality model

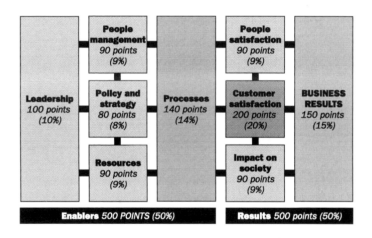

The nine components indicated in the model are categorised as Enablers and Results. Consistently achieving high standards for Enablers produces excellence in business results.

Apart from the European quality award there is also a UK quality award managed by The British Quality Foundation using the European Quality Model.

## Uses of European Quality Model – be creative!

1. One can use the model to bring about a balanced measurement system. Performance indicators of each enabler can be formulated and performance measured accordingly. For example, if one takes the leadership dimension, its effectiveness can be measured by finding out what kind of commitment a leader has? How is this commitment perceived by all employees? Is the mission statement and corporate objectives communicated to all throughout the organisation? How is this communicated? What role does top management play in total quality initiatives? How do the employees of an organisation rate their leaders? etc.

    One could do similar assessments in relation to processes, systems, managing people and satisfying customers. Such measurements will give balanced perspective.

2. The model can also be used as a benchmarking framework. Each enabler can be benchmarked against competitors or partners to bring about best practice in an organisation.

# ISO 9000

Many organisations seek ISO 9000 registration to embark upon quality improvement initiative. The standards deal with quality assurance. The ISO 9000 has the following three parts:

1. **ISO 9001.** This is the model for quality assurance in design, development, production, installation and servicing.

2. **ISO 9002.** This is the model for quality assurance in production, installation and servicing.

3. **ISO 9003.** This is the model for quality assurance in final inspection and test.

Each of the ISO 9000 assessment standards contain 20 criteria which provide a guide to designing an effective quality management system.

## How to design an effective quality management system

*Step 1*

▶ Evaluation of existing quality procedures against the requirements of the ISO standards.

▶ Introduce performance measures at this stage.

▶ Design a system to gather information.

*Step 2*

▶ Identify key staff and train them. These staff members will be responsible for implementation.

▶ Select internal auditors and train them.

*Step 3*

▶ Carry out regular internal audits.

▶ Identify corrective actions needed to conform with ISO standards.

*Step 4*

▶ Prepare a quality assurance programme.

▶ Definition, documentation and implementation of new procedures.

▶ Communicate to all employees.

*Step 5*

▶ Preparation of a quality manual.

▶ Pre-assessment meeting with registrar to analyse quality manual.

*Step 6*

▶ Assessment visit.

▶ Certification.

## How to succeed in implementing a quality initiative

▶ Set realistic goals.

▶ Do not initiate project as a window dressing exercise.

▶ Have conviction and commitment in what you propose to do.

▶ Focus on customer satisfaction as the end result.

▶ Minimise bureaucracy.

▶ Articulate your company values very clearly.

▶ Train your staff.

▶ Do not use quality initiative to downsize your organisation.

▶ Align your quality initiative with your corporate strategy.

▶ Provide strong and effective leadership.

## Be effective not simply efficient

In business, a distinction is drawn between being effective and being efficient. Being effective is doing the right thing right while being efficient is doing things right. Effectiveness relates to achieving the objectives set. In relation to the analysis tool (opposite), the quality company should aim to position itself in segment A.

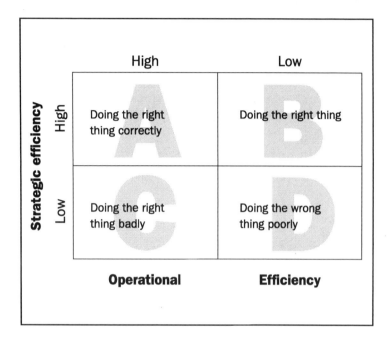

# Managing the environment

### Do you care for your environment?

In most cases total quality now embraces environmental considerations. Avoiding waste, saving energy, making better use of material, recycling etc leads to a reduction in costs, operational efficiency and the creation of new technologies. Environmental considerations should be the concern of all business big and small. The series of ISO 1400 standards were introduced in 1996 to enhance environmental performance in business.

## TOOL BOX 22 TWENTY-TWO

### How to adopt and implement an environmental management system

1.  Make a commitment to protect the environment and prepare an environmental policy.

2.  Put the organisation and system in place and appoint personnel responsible for implementing and monitoring environmental factors.

3.  Monitor implementation and operation.

4.  Undertake an environmental audit. This involves measuring what has been achieved and measuring the effectiveness of the systems or management processes which are or have been used to achieve them.

5.  Take corrective action for unfavourable variances.

6.  Review your management system.

# CHAPTER 6SIX

# Managing and dealing with finance

# Managing and dealing with finance

**ALL BUSINESSES HAVE** to deal with finance. After organisations have prepared their strategies they then have to prepare strategic objectives. Each department or section or region then have to prepare their objectives which have to be consistent with the organisation's objectives. Associated with objectives are performance indicators to monitor these objectives. Generally speaking these indicators are financial in their characteristics. Costs, profits, return on capital employed, price earning ratio etc are all indicators which have financial characteristics.

In commercial business, there are three sources of financial information. These are Balance Sheets, Profit and Loss Statements and Sources and Application of Funds.

## Balance Sheet

A Balance Sheet is a financial situation of an organisation showing what an organisation owes (its liabilities) and what it owns (its assets). It is a statement of total assets and liabilities of a business at a particular moment in time. In other words, it is a financial snapshot of the business.

## Profit and Loss Statement

Profit and Loss Account shows how the company has traded in the year it is reporting. The account includes revenue and expenditure items which relate to the year under consideration and these items are matched to calculate profit and loss. Profit is the excess of sales revenue over the costs incurred in achieving that sales revenue.

### Sources and application of funds

This statement shows where the money in the business has come from (issue of shares, borrowing etc) and how it has been spent or applied (investment in fixed assets and working capital).

# Managing your working capital

The management of working capital is the lifeblood of any business. **Profits do not equal cash.** Working capital is current assets minus current liabilities. Working capital is needed to keep business afloat.

Businesses incur expenses in terms of buying raw materials, holding stocks etc and at the same time it receives money from buyers. The gap between incurring expenditure and receiving cash is very important to manage. The longer you pay your supplier and the shorter the period you allow for your customers to pay you would lead to less working capital. If the time you pay your supplier is longer than the time you receive money from customers then you need more working capital. Your working capital will also be very small if you do not hold stocks or you hold stocks for a very short period.

A business makes profit by selling its products and service but if not enough cash is generated to meet its obligations, it becomes insolvent.

## TOOL BOX 23 TWENTY-THREE

### How to manage your working capital

▶ Negotiate long credit terms with your suppliers.

▶ Negotiate short credit terms with your customers.

▶ Make sure the credit terms you negotiate with your suppliers are longer than the terms negotiated with your customers.

▶ Hold less stocks but not at the expense of affecting delivery promise.

▶ Control your cash effectively.

▶ Managing working capital involves controlling your debtors, creditors and your stock, including work-in-progress

▶ Do not delay sending out invoices. If sending abroad, make sure what the custom of the country you are dealing with is in terms of payment period.

▶ Make it easy for customers to place orders.

▶ Make sure your stock profile is consistent with your sales order profile.

▶ Monitor disputed invoices and make sure they are settled as soon as possible.

▶ Budget for stock and constantly monitor stock levels.

▶ Make sure that stocks recorded actually exist.

▶ Monitor the system of processing an item from order to delivery.

▶ Reduce work-in-progress time.

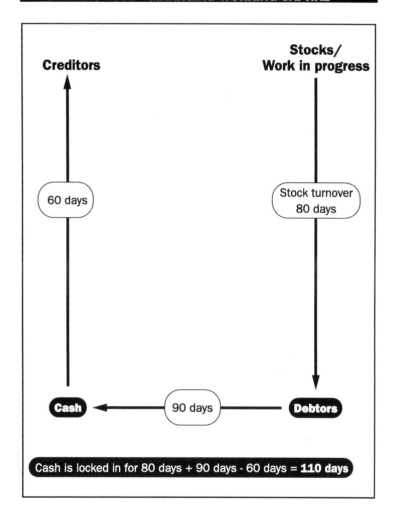

**Creditors**

**Stocks/
Work in progress**

60 days

Stock turnover
80 days

Cash ← 90 days — Debtors

Cash is locked in for 80 days + 90 days - 60 days = **110 days**

### Conducting break-even analysis

The main object of doing break-even analysis is to make sure that your total sales revenue equals total costs. When your sales revenue is in excess of your total costs you make profit. Profit could be calculated at gross level or at net level. Gross profit excludes overhead costs whereas net profit includes overhead costs.

In working out break-even analysis you want to make sure that your gross profit or the gross margin you generate from your sales is sufficient to cover your overheads or fixed costs.

For example, let us assume that variable costs for your business are £50,000 per year and your fixed costs (overheads) are £25,000. You have the capacity to produce 10,000 units of product 'X'. To cover variable and fixed costs (total costs) you need to sell 10,000 units of 'X' at £7.50 each.

This is your break-even point (£75,000/10,000 = £7.50)

To sell 10,000 units at £7.50 will generate £75,000. Your gross profit margin is gross profit x 100/75,000 = gross margin %.

In this case it will be 25,000 x 100/75,000 = 33.3%

The other aspect of finance is understanding various ratios and what they mean. Such understanding will enable you to interpret your business accounts.

# Key financial ratios

### Return on capital employed

Profit/capital employed. Capital employed is total assets minus current assets.

### Asset turnover

Sales/capital employed. This figure will indicate the frequency with which assets have been converted into sales during the accounting period.

Both the above ratios are measure of return on investment.

### Profit margin

Profit before interest payable and tax/sales.

Profit margin provides information on how a business is managing its operating costs.

### Gross margin

Gross profit/sales.

The figure shows the contribution towards overheads.

### Asset turnover

Sales/capital employed.

The figure will show the frequency with which assets have been converted into sales during the accounting period.

In managing working capital the three key ratios are stock turnover, debtor turnover and creditor turnover.

## Stock turnover

Cost of goods sold/closing stock.

This figure shows how quickly goods move through the business.

## Debtor days

Debtors/cost of sales x 365.

The figure shows the number of days' sales for which payment is outstanding.

## Creditor days

Trade creditors/cost of sales x 365.

This will show the number of days' purchases for which payment is still due.

How solvent is your business? The appropriate ratios are the acid ratio, current ratio and the debt ratio.

## Acid test

Liquid assets/current liabilities.

This shows the liquidity position of your business.

## Current ratio

Current assets/current liabilities.

This shows to what extent your short-term assets are adequate to cover your short-term liabilities.

### Debt ratio

Debt/capital employed.

The low debt ratio is an indication of high level of safety.

If your business is trading in the Stock Market then you also have to consider earning per share ratio, price earning ratio and dividend cover.

### Earning per share

Profit after tax/number of ordinary shares in issue.

Many analysts use this measure to reflect business performance.

### Price/earning ratio

Market price per share/earning per share.

### Dividend cover

Earning per share/dividends per share.

This figure shows the number of times dividends could have been paid out of the current year's earnings.

The key ratios highlighted can reveal a lot of information on business performance.

# Managing shareholder value

Stern Stewart & Co., the New York management consultants developed and popularised the concepts of Economic Value Added (EVA) and Market Value Added (MVA) in order to assess shareholder value. In an article *Creating stockholder wealth* by Anne B Fisher

(*Fortune*, 11 December, 1995), she explains MVA as 'a measure of the wealth a company has created for investors. MVA in effect shows the difference between what investors put in and what they can take out. MVA is supposed to be a good performance indicator of whether the company has made a profit for its investors.

Economic Value Added (EVA) is after-tax net operating profit minus cost of capital. A positive EVA often signifies a strong stock.

# Budgetary control

Once the strategy has been determined and strategic objectives formulated, an organisation then prepares an overall corporate budget. Without preparing a budget it is difficult to measure the performance of an organisation. The corporate budget is sometimes known as the master budget.

From master budget, divisional or sectional or regional budgets are then prepared. Guidelines regarding inflation, employee numbers, key targets relating to growth and margins are often set by top management or negotiated with top management.

Budgets include information on revenues, cost of sales, gross margin, overhead costs and net margins. Once budgets have been accepted the flow of costs, revenues, and expenditure is scheduled. Budget holders receive regular information on theses flows and they have to explain any variances that occur in report format. Analysis of variances (the difference between budgeted targets and actual targets) enable budget holders to take appropriate corrective action.

Some organisations have **zero-based budgeting systems** which assumes starting from scratch each year having done all the appropriate analyses while other organisations **have historical budgeting system** which takes into consideration prior years results.

# CHAPTER 7SEVEN

# Making decisions

# Making decisions

**DECISIONS BECOME PART** of our life whether we are in business or not. In business we have to make decisions about deciding on our strategy, our markets, people we employ, systems we buy, resources we invest in and so on.

A human brain has two sides. The left side of our brain controls a significant proportion of analytical mental functions and it houses rational and logical capabilities. The right side of our brain, on the other hand, involves intuitive capabilities. The left side tends to process information in a sequential manner, whereas, the right side tends to deal with simultaneous relations.

Some experts tell us that most people have bias towards one side or the other. Making decisions involve the use of both sides of the brain. The left side enables us to make decisions based on facts and logic, whereas, the right side enables us to make decisions on intuition, 'gut feel' or emotions.

People deal with information in a specific way. They gradually develop their own unique style of making decisions.

M. Driver and J. Lintott (*Managerial Decision Diagnostics*, 1972) categorised decision styles into (a) the Decisive Style, (b) the Flexible Style, (c) the Hierarchic Style and (d) the Integrative Style.

## The Decisive Style

This type of person does not use data very much. This person knows what he or she wants to do as he/she is focused towards his/her objectives. This person is not interested in building scenarios towards long-term planning. He/she feels comfortable in a situation of rules and procedures. He/she is focused on single outcome.

## The Flexible Style

This type of person also does not use data very much but he/she focuses on the different goals he or she wants to achieve. He does not plan for contingencies. His reasoning shifts according to the situation he/she is facing. The Flexible prefers not to be in charge but will do so, if necessary.

## The Hierarchic Style

This person prefers to handle a lot of data with a single focus in mind. His/her tactic is to use as much information as possible in order to achieve a precise goal he/she has set. This person makes a contingency plan to cover various possibilities. He/she is a methodical problem solver.

## The Integrative Style

This person uses a lot of information and he/she like to experiment. He/she does not have set opinions. This person is often very creative and likes to involve other people in seeking solutions.

People do not fall neatly into the four categories highlighted but one or two styles of making decisions dominate in individuals. Knowing the dominant decision styles of your employees help to allocate projects and build teams.

# Decision-making techniques

Irrespective of your styles, there are various techniques and models available in arriving at certain decisions. If an organisation has faced a situation often enough in the past, then they can develop a manual of making decision if similar situations develop in the future.

When you make a decision you are using two major resources: these are information and judgement. If you make a wrong decision, the cause must lie with either your information or your judgement or both.

---

**TOOL BOX 25TWENTY-FIVE**

### How to make a structured decision

1.  State what problem you are facing.

2.  Diagnose and analyse the causes of this problem.

3.  Develop alternative solutions.

4.  Write down pros and cons of each alternative.

5.  Select the solution that meets your current need. Remember the alternative you choose does not have to be the one with the most 'pros'.

6.  If you cannot have the best solution make the best of what you have.

7.  Implement the chosen solution.

8.  Get feedback to assess the results of your implementation.

9.  Has the solution produced desired result? If yes, you have resolved your problem. If not, you have to take corrective action.

---

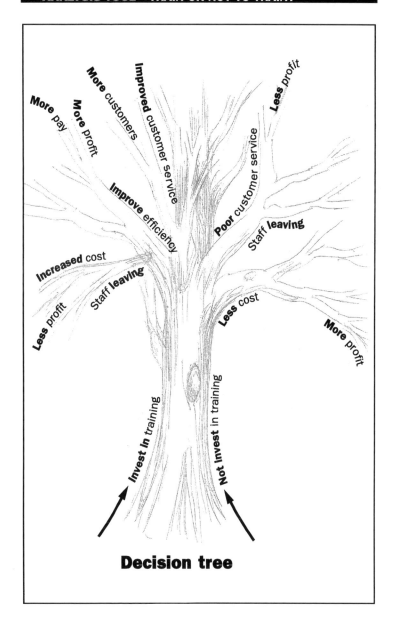

**Decision tree**

In business it is often a matter of choosing between alternatives. If you are launching a product you may have an option of spending a lot of money at launch stage to promote your product or you might promote your product gradually. You have to assess the consequences of the two alternative actions looked at. The outcomes of actions or decisions and the alternatives can be set out as a 'Decision tree'. (See p.83.)

It is always better to involve key employees in the decision-making process. Doing so will enable your staff to acquire a better insight into your business and come up with creative solutions. In some situations businesses conduct brainstorming sessions to solve problems. **Brainstorming** involves a face-to-face interactive group spontaneously suggesting ideas for problem solving. Participants are encouraged to come up with ideas to resolve problems regardless of their likelihood of being implemented. The main objective of brainstorming is to encourage flexible thinking and creativity.

# CHAPTER 8EIGHT

## Managing performance

# Managing performance

**IN ORDER TO** survive and compete effectively, every business – big or small – has to measure and manage its performance. In the past, attention has been focused on financial measurement. Revenues, cost of sales gross profit, overhead costs and net profit are the key financial measurement. These measures will continue to exist because at the end of the day commercial businesses want to make profit for themselves, their partners and where appropriate, their shareholders.

However, in the past five years businesses have been urged to consider other stakeholders such as employees, customers, and to measure what extent their needs are met. It is said that **profit follows customer satisfaction**.

There are in practice a family of measures. There are quantitative measures such as staff turnover rate, absenteeism rate, profit per employee, time to delivery, accidents per projects etc and qualitative measures such as staff morale, discrimination, leadership and work illness. Then there are financial measures such as gross and net profit, revenue per product or region, costs and so on and non-financial measures such as hospital waiting lists, defect rate, and so on.

Many organisations use a combination of qualitative, quantitative, financial and non-financial measures.

## Arrival of balanced scorecard

In 1992, Professor Robert Kaplan of Harvard Business School and Dr. David P. Norton of the Renaissance Strategy Group introduced the balanced scorecard approach which is now becoming very popular with many organisations. The scorecard incorporates measurement involving customers, shareholders, employees, processes and learning.

Focus is put on the following four perspectives:

**Financial perspectives**: Examples, return on capital employed, cash flow, liquidity, product profitability etc.

**Customer perspective**: Examples, market share, on-time delivery, defect rate, lead time etc.

**Process perspective**: Examples: safety, Time to market, project performance etc.

**Growth and learning perspective**: Examples, revenue per employee, rate of technological development, new product development, employees development etc.

Some organisations have singled out employees from a growth and learning perspective and focus attention on employee perspective separately. What perspectives you employ and focus attention on will depend on the nature of your business.

Assuming you are interested in a balanced scorecard approach what should you do?

---

**TOOL BOX 26 TWENTY-SIX**

**Adopting a balanced scorecard approach**

The centre piece of any balanced scorecard is your business strategy. It does not matter what perspectives you adopt, your organisation or business strategy must drive and determine the perspectives and measures you adopt.

*See over*

---

## STEP 1

### Strategy and vision

Articulate your business strategy and vision. What is your business trying to achieve now and in the foreseeable future?

_____

_____

_____

## STEP 2

### Financial perspectives

What financial measures are crucial to your business? Formulate measures to meet what is required.

_____

_____

_____

## STEP 3

### Customer perspective

What do customers expect from us? Formulate measures that will tell you if you are meeting their expectations.

_____

_____

_____

## STEP 4

**Business processes**

What processes do we have in order to add value in our production? Analyse activities involved in each process.

_____

_____

_____

_____

## STEP 5

**Organisational learning and innovation**

What do we need to do in terms of our capabilities and competencies in order to compete effectively?

_____

_____

_____

Some organisations have decided to adopt the European Quality Model and use enablers to formulate measures of their performance. Such an approach also will bring about a multi-focus measurement system if that is the sort of measurement system which you think is appropriate for your organisation.

**The important thing is not to follow any business fad but to make judgements in relation to the needs of your business or organisation.**

In considering balanced measurements remember to link financial measures to corporate strategy, consider staff development and re-skilling, succession planning, team approach, listening to customers, delivering service excellence, customer retention, quality, reducing cycle time, reducing costs and new product introduction.

# CHAPTER 9NINE

# Managing meetings

# Managing meetings

> *'A committee is a group that keeps
> the minutes and loses the hours.'*    **Source: Unknown**

> *'The length of a meeting rises with the square
> of the number of people present.'*    **Source: Unknown**

**MEETINGS! MEETINGS, MEETINGS!** They have become part of our life. It is said that meetings are as inevitable in the business world as 'death and taxes' and just about as popular.

## Reasons for holding meetings:

- To gather and give information.
- To get advice.
- To resolve a problem.
- To negotiate.
- To consult.

The amount of control the chairman exerts over the meeting will depend on the type of meeting. Meetings operate at formal as well as informal levels; there will be personal interests of people involved and their hidden agendas.

### How to prepare for a meeting

▶ You must decide on the agenda showing the items to be covered.

▶ You should indicate on the agenda items for information and items for discussion.

▶ If possible indicate time to be allocated to each item.

▶ Decide who should attend the meeting.

▶ Decide on the room layout.

▶ Look at possible outcomes.

## Chairman's role at the meeting

- Opening the meeting and going over the agenda.

- Controlling the whole process of the meeting.

- Sticking to the agenda.

- Facilitating discussions.

- Getting appropriate decisions.

- Closing.

At the meeting all members have responsibilities for making certain that the meeting is a success. They should understand the objectives of the meeting and undertake appropriate pre-meeting preparation.

# Interpersonal skills required to run a meeting

### Feelings

- Respect and acknowledge emotions.
- Be aware of the 'hidden agenda'.
- Pay attention to the language and in particular body language.
- Direct the behaviour of participants.

### Conflict resolution

- Agree on what has been decided. Clarify areas of disagreements.
- Explain what will be done in relation to disagreed items.
- Aim for consensus.
- Use assertiveness skills.
- Be positive.

### Problem-solving

- Get information.
- Share information.
- Provide support.
- Aim to get results.

Managing meetings is about managing people in groups. Some people talk more easily than others in groups. Some individuals bring hidden agendas to meetings. These hidden agendas are a set of personal objectives which very often have nothing to do with objectives of group meetings.

## The type of people you may encounter in a meeting

- The silent one.
- The hostile one.
- The one who goes on and on.
- The suggestion maker.
- The devil's advocate.
- The wondering nomad.
- The side-conversationalist.
- The know-all.
- The sleeping partner.

**The challenge to the chairman is to manage this diversity.**

The process of a meeting undergoes four stages of development. They are **Forming** when the chairman is trying to set rapport with members. **Storming** when personal agendas are revealed. **Norming** when the direction is set and procedures are followed and **Performing** when the group reaches a maturity stage to address the issues and come to a resolution. The stages of group development and the time associated with each stage will depend on the type of meeting, the number of people in the meeting, the effectiveness of the chairman and the objectives to be achieved.

The purpose of a group is to perform specific tasks (meeting objectives as per the agenda). Each individual member within the group has a different degree of commitment to the task. In managing a meeting it is important to distinguish between content and process. Content refers to subject matter under discussion or to the tasks to be performed and the process is the way content is handled. The chairman has to be competent in content as well as the process aspect of managing a meeting.

## Remember

- Ineffective meetings are caused by an unclear purpose, inappropriate style adopted by a chairman, lack of control and inadequate preparation.

- Managing a meeting involves questioning, facilitating group formation, listening, participation, observation, open communication, defusing conflict, decision-making and achieving objectives.

- Things that go wrong in the meeting involve time-wasting, backtracking, lack of participation, lack of commitment, interruptions, dominance by some members, red herrings, and poor or break down in communication.

- Meetings involve business investment in people, time and money. You should evaluate each meeting after it is over to assess payback of this investment.

- Do the follow-up after the meeting. Who is to do what and by when?

**How well do you manage a meeting?**

| Answer 'Yes' or 'No' as appropriate | Yes | No |
|---|---|---|
| 1. I hate meetings. | ☐ | ☐ |
| 2. I think meetings are a waste of time. | ☐ | ☐ |
| 3. Meeting agendas should be prepared well in advance. | ☐ | ☐ |
| 4. Meeting agendas should be circulated well in advance before the meeting. | ☐ | ☐ |
| 5. Meeting documentation should be circulated to members at least one week in advance. | ☐ | ☐ |
| 6. The chairman should explain the purpose of the meeting in advance of the meeting. | ☐ | ☐ |
| 7. Meetings should be well controlled. | ☐ | ☐ |
| 8. All members should be allowed to make contributions. | ☐ | ☐ |
| 9. Those who hog the meeting should be asked by the chairman not to do so. | ☐ | ☐ |
| 10. Those who go on and on at the meeting should not be invited to the meeting again. | ☐ | ☐ |
| 11. The chairman should stick to finishing agenda items and not pay attention to the behaviour of the members. | ☐ | ☐ |
| 12. The chairman's style should always be autocratic. | ☐ | ☐ |
| 13. The chairman should not allow side conversations. | ☐ | ☐ |
| 14. Meetings are about time management and nothing else. | ☐ | ☐ |
| 15. The chairman should be neutral and not influence the meeting. | ☐ | ☐ |

## How well can you manage a meeting?

Answer 'Yes' or 'No' as appropriate          **Yes**     **No**

**16**. A chairman is the only person responsible for the outcome of the meeting. ☐ ☐

**17**. Some people at the meetings do not say anything. ☐ ☐

**18**. A chairman should facilitate the outcome of the meeting. ☐ ☐

**19**. There is a need to analyse all meetings once they are finished. ☐ ☐

**20**. The chairman's job is over once the meeting is finished. ☐ ☐

## Scoring

| *Questions* | *Answers* |
|---|---|
| 1-2 | Give 2 points for 'No' and 1 point for 'Yes'. |
| 3-8 | Give 1 point for 'No' and 2 points for 'Yes'. |
| 9-12 | Give 2 points for 'No' and 1 point for 'Yes'. |
| 13 | Give 1 point for 'No' and 2 points for 'Yes'. |
| 14-16 | Give 2 points for 'No' and 1 point for 'Yes'. |
| 17-19 | Give 1 point for 'No' and 2 points for 'Yes'. |
| 20 | Give 2 points for 'No' and 1 point for 'Yes'. |

**40-36 points**.  Excellent.

**35-32 points**.  Very Good.

**Under 31 points**. You have to improve your meeting management skill.

# CHAPTER 10TEN

# Managing time effectively

# Managing time effectively

> *'Time is the scarcest resource and unless it is managed, nothing else can be managed.'* **Peter Drucker**

**TIME MANAGEMENT IS** usually talked about within the context of work and especially managerial work. The main objective is to manage time in order to be effective in what you do. It is said that we spend most of our life 'doing things right rather than doing the right things.'

It is important to manage time not only within the context of work but also to manage time in order to enhance personal life and materialise personal aspirations and goals.

Time management is a situational factor. To what extent you can get organised depends on the work you do, the organisation and the boss you work for, your personality, your age and your culture. The techniques of managing time are easily understood but it is applying them that needs determination and self-discipline.

---

### ANALYSIS TOOL · WHAT TIME MEANS TO YOU

**Write down in a few words what time means to you.**

_____

_____

_____

_____

---

What time means to you will influence your thinking and behaviour. Do remember time is a measure of your life. Managing time leads to managing your life. This is not being philosophical but being pragmatic.

Every person is faced with numerous choices every day. One has to do many things involving different people at work and at home and all these people make demands on your time. In one day you have to allocate time as a boss, as a colleague, as a team member, as brother, as father, as husband or wife, as friend and so on. Every choice and decision made involves what is called an 'opportunity cost'.

An opportunity cost is a sacrificed alternative. If you give more time to your work you will have less time for your non-work activities. Similarly, if you spend more time on less important work then you will have less time left for important work.

## An opportunity cost

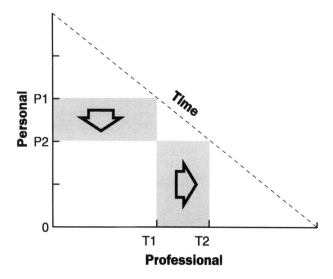

An opportunity cost of extra professional time is P1 – P2

## ANALYSIS TOOL · HOW YOU SPEND YOUR TIME

**How do you spend your time, say over a typical week?**

| Activities | Hours | % of time |
|---|---|---|
| Work | | |
| Travel inc. commuting | | |
| Sleep | | |
| Personal | | |

Some people like to organise themselves while others enjoy the excitement of an unplanned day. In fact there is no need to manage your time if you have no problem or if you do not know where you want to go in your life.

Assuming that one has aspirations and personal and professional goals to achieve, it is very important to view time as a composite resource.

**List five goals you want to achieve in your professional life and five goals in your personal life.**

*Professional*

1. _____

2. _____

3. _____

4. _____

5. _____

*Personal*

1. _____

2. _____

3. _____

4. _____

5. _____

---

ANALYSIS TOOL · **YOUR TOP GOALS**

**Select three top goals in your personal life and three top goals in your professional life and make a plan.**

Planning involves asking the following questions and coming up with answers:

**WHAT** is it you want to achieve?

**WHY** do you want to achieve them?

**WHEN** do you want to achieve them?

**HOW** do you want to go about achieving them?

Maybe you have never had an opportunity to focus your attention on what it is you would like to achieve in your life. Possibly you may have thought about your career development and career planning but not life planning as such. So start now and reap the benefits.

## ANALYSIS TOOL · PREPARING YOUR OBJECTIVES

Prepare objectives for your goal. In other words, against each objective write what objectives you propose to achieve as a result of meeting your goal. Make sure these objectives are realistic and attainable and you can put a time frame to them.

Example:

My goal is _____

_____

My objective for achieving this goal is _____

_____

## ANALYSIS TOOL · ACHIEVING YOUR GOALS

### How do I go about achieving my goals?

Having decided **what** your goals are and what objectives you want to achieve and having decided **when** you want to achieve these goals, your next step is to decide **how** you are going to go about achieving them. At this stage you will need to decide your tactics and prepare your plan highlighting various activities involved towards reaching your goals.

## Improving your time management at work

1. Make a list of all activities from the time you arrive at work to the time leave for home.

2. Group these activities according to 'Essential tasks,' 'Routine tasks,' 'Previous commitments,' 'Interruptions'.

   From this analysis you will get a good idea of the volume of interruptions you are handling daily, the spill over work and the routine work.

3. Prioritise all your activities according to what is **important** and what is **urgent**. You are paid to be effective not busy. This is what is meant by 'work smart not hard'.

**Urgent**: Things you must do now.

They may or may not relate to your objectives but you have to do them. Neglecting urgent tasks create crises.

**Important**: Activities which contribute to your goals.

4. With reference to the figure overleaf, your first priority will be to attend to tasks that fall in box A. Then Box B and C.

5. Use your peak time to attend items in Box A and Box B.

6. Analyse interruptions. Are they part of your work? Can you minimise them?

7. Everyday prepare a list of 'Things I must do' and 'Things I want to do'.

8. Always reserve some time as uncommitted time.

9. Group activities. For example, set time aside for attending to your correspondence, making sales calls etc. Batching activities leads to saving time.

10. Group activities that give you a high pay-off.

11. Visit Mr. Talkative in his office or area then you can leave easily.

No matter how busy you are, you should always take time to plan. Time management it is said is common sense but it takes a knowledge of techniques and method to turn common sense into common practice.

Planning your time on a daily basis is like forming a habit. Habits are behaviours that have been performed so often that they have become mechanical or automatic. Psychologist William James suggested the following approach to changing or forming habits:

**Step 1.** Launch the new behaviours as strongly as possible.

**Step 2.** Seize the first opportunity to act on the new behaviour.

**Step 3.** Never let an exception occur until the new behaviour is firmly rooted.

## Priority analysis

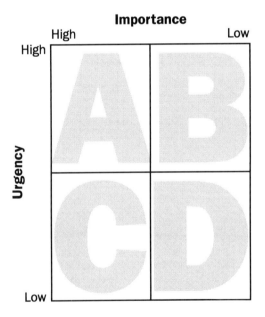

# Steps to habit formation

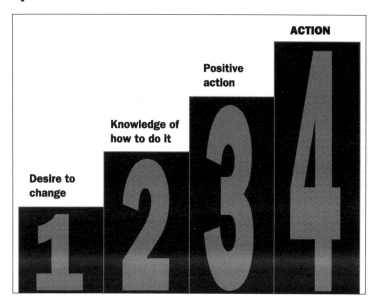

▲ ▲ ▲ ▲ ▲ ▲ ▲ ▲ ▲ ▲ ▲ ▲ ▲ ▲ ▲ ▲ ▲

# CHAPTER 11ELEVEN

# Managing people

▼ ▼ ▼ ▼        ▼

# Managing people

## Leadership, motivation and performance

Most organisations declare in their Annual Reports that their staff are their biggest asset and yet most of them have very little consideration for their people. People in organisations should be considered as an appreciating asset. Managing people is the most challenging function of any manager.

### What does managing people involve?

It involves:

- providing effective leadership
- recruiting, motivating, developing and retaining good staff
- having an honest and open communication
- trusting staff
- coaching and counselling
- respecting staff.

Staff have to be managed so that they develop 'I am OK. You're OK' feeling. The culture of the organisation should be such that staff develop high concern for their organisations as well as for themselves. (See opposite).

# I am OK syndrome

**Concern for self**

|  | High | Low |
|---|---|---|
| **High** | I am not OK<br>You're OK | I am OK<br>You're OK |
| **Low** | I am not OK<br>You're not OK | I am OK<br>You're not OK |

**Concern for organisation**

## TOOL BOX 29 TWENTY-NINE

### How to provide effective leadership

▶ Have a vision for your business and make sure you communicate it to all concerned.

▶ Serve your staff who in turn can serve customers.

▶ Have a conviction and commitment in your ability to lead.

▶ Institutionalise trust in your organisation.

▶ Communicate openly and honestly with all your staff.

▶ Be supportive.

▶ Be imaginative and innovative.

▶ Do not sacrifice your staff during the time of crisis.

▶ Be accessible to your staff.

▶ Behave ethically.

▶ Be socially responsible for your actions.

▶ Make a commitment to train and develop your staff.

▶ Be a good listener.

## TOOL BOX 30THIRTY

### Recruiting – factors to consider

1. What kind of competencies and skills do you require?

2. Do you have such competencies and skills in your organisation?

3. What do you want to achieve in recruiting ?

4. Do the skills you want match the job for which you are recruiting?

5. Do you want this person to update his or her skills as their job expands or changes?

6. What type of a person would be suitable for a job? Prepare a profile.

7. Would this person, apart from having an appropriate skill, work well with other staff?

8. What kind of responsibilities do you want this person to have?

9. Are you willing to empower him and is he or she willing to take responsibility?

10. How are you going to recruit?

11. What information will you provide to applicants for the job?

12. Who is going to recruit?

13. Who will be involved in the selection process?

14. What are you willing to offer?

15. What type of induction training are you going to have?

It is very important at the recruitment stage to have mission and strategic objectives. Before the job is offered, the successful candidate should be in the picture as to what that person is expected to do, what kind of skill he/she is expected to have, why the organisation is interested in specific skills, what are the strategic objectives of the whole organisation in the short-term and middle-term and what part a successful candidate is expected to play.

Open and honest information, provided at the recruitment stage, will motivate the candidate and will reduce staff turnover because in many cases organisations at recruitment stage hype the positioning and objectives of their organisations thus creating frustrations which leads to staff leaving.

**Tool box 31** (opposite) structures the thinking and enables managers to do appropriate preparation and avoid costly mistakes. The framework is also a guide to best practice recruitment.

# Interviewing

Interviewing for selection is the most important occasion. Organisations have to select candidates who are going to bring in their skills and experience in order to enable organisations to achieve their objectives. It is important at the interview to assess candidates' personality, their education, their experience, their aspirations and their motivation to work.

For such an important occasion some people involved in interview selection do no or very little preparation. Some try to read information literally a few minutes before a selection interview and some while they are interviewing. What is lacking from an organisation's point of view is the understanding of the importance of selection interviews.

## Preparing for a selection interview

▶ Read all the information sent to you by candidates.

▶ Make key points of what attracted you to call this specific candidate for an interview.

▶ Assess the candidate's educational qualifications and prepare a list of things you would like to clarify.

▶ Assess the candidate's experience and find out their previous achievements at work.

▶ Send the information about the company and about the job well before the interview.

▶ Make arrangements as to where the interview is going to take place.

▶ When the candidate arrives treat him or her with respect.

▶ Make the candidate at ease and establish rapport.

▶ Make it clear that the interview is a two-way flow. You are trying assess the candidate and the candidate should be given an opportunity to assess you.

▶ Allow adequate time to explore all the factors and the issues.

▶ Give the candidate a chance to talk about their references and the referees they have chosen.

▶ Take an opportunity to find out how candidate's aspirations can be reconciled with corporate and departmental/divisional objectives.

▶ Do not play games or tricks on the candidate. You are there to get the best information about the candidate.

▶ Facilitate information flow.

▶ Be courteous.

Having made the selection it is very important to prepare induction training for the candidate. This is not done well by many organisations due to lack of time, resources and consideration. Investment in training at an early stage will subsequently pay good dividends.

# Motivation

Motivating staff is the biggest challenge any business faces. Within the context of intensive competition and many changes that are taking place in the business environment how can businesses motivate their staff? With so much cost-cutting, downsizing (some businesses are capsizing) and various change initiatives that are taking place how can employees feel secure? Some businesses also expect their employees to manage their own career development and prospects of vertical promotions have become rare.

Management literature provides guidance to various theories of motivation ranging from job rewards and job design to meeting the expectations of employees.

### Maslow's Theory of Need

Maslow's theory is referred to as his 'Hierarchy of Human Needs' (*Toward a Psychology of Being*, 1962) because he arranges the needs under certain headings as follows:

**Survival needs**: This is low level needs incorporating food, air, water.

**Security needs**: This next level of needs incorporating security of employment and generally the need for self-preservation.

**Social needs**: There is a need for love, belonging, peer acceptance.

**Ego needs**: This is a higher level need involving the needs for self-respect, self-esteem, autonomy, achievement, and a need to command respect and status.

**Self-actualisation needs**: The highest level of need which relates to personal growth and achievement

# Hierarchy of needs

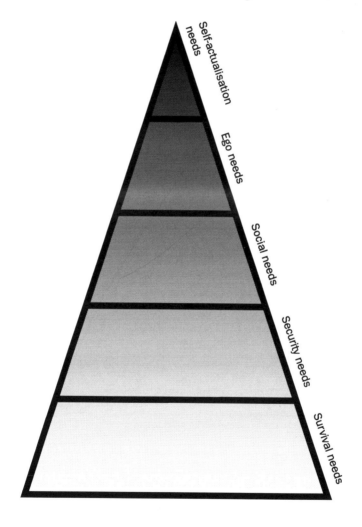

## Herzberg's Two Factor Theory

Frederick Herzberg found that there are two important factors at work (*The Motivation to Work*, 1964). The first set of factors he labelled as hygiene factors and the second set of factors he labelled as motivation factors.

**Hygiene factors** relate to conditions of work and are sources of dissatisfaction. They can have a negative effect on performance.

**Motivation factors** relate to the content of the job and are sources of work satisfaction. However, their absence does not create dissatisfaction.

| **Motivators**: | **Hygiene factors**: |
|---|---|
| Achievement | Company policy |
| Recognition | Supervision |
| Work itself | Working conditions |
| Responsibility | Salary |
| Advancement | Status |
| Growth | Job security |

## McClelland's Theory of Need Achievement

According to this theory, motivation is based upon three distinct needs. These are:

**Need for Power**: Basic drive to control and direct others.

**Need for Affiliation**: The need for friendship, personal relationships and social interaction.

**Need for Achievement**: The need to attain goals.

## Expectancy Theory

This theory was put forward by Victor Vroom (*Work and Motivation*, 1964) and has had an influence on thinking on motivation. According to Vroom, there is a relationship between the level of motivation, the importance of a goal (valence which is the value or worth) and the expectation of achieving it.

**ANALYSIS TOOL · HOW TO MOTIVATE**

There is no universally accepted motivation theory. It is important to remember that all people are different and that managers cannot always motivate people. They can, however, provide an environment and an opportunity for people to gain a high level of motivation at work.

When people join any organisation, apart from having a legal contract there is also what is now known as a **psychological contract**. Organisations have certain expectations of those they recruit but those recruited also have certain expectations.

## Motivation and psychological contract

| **What the individual may expect to receive and the organisation may expect to give**. | **What the individual may expect to give and the organisation may expect to receive**. |
|---|---|
| Salary | An honest day's work |
| Personal development | Loyalty |
| Recognition/Approval | Initiative |
| Security | Conformity |
| Conducive environment | Job effectiveness |
| Fairness | Flexibility |
| Meaningful job | Willingness to learn and develop |

## ANALYSIS TOOL · PERFORMANCE EXPECTATION

▶ What do my staff expect from my organisation?

_____

_____

▶ Do I meet these expectations?

_____

_____

▶ What do I expect from my staff?

_____

_____

▶ Do they meet my expectation?

_____

_____

▶ Are there any gaps?

_____

_____

▶ What are these gaps?

_____

_____

▶ How can we close these gaps?

_____

_____

▶ Who should do what?

_____

_____

### How to motivate your staff

▶ Communicate your vision and goals openly and honestly.

▶ Involve your employees in preparing their own objectives in relation to their work.

▶ Indicate where and how their performance will impact on business goals.

▶ Make their work meaningful by relating their activities and performance to strategy.

▶ Monitor their performance regularly and reward good performance.

▶ Help your employees to acquire new skills.

▶ Provide opportunities for training.

▶ Counsel and coach them to achieve set objectives.

▶ Show them that you do care for their welfare at work.

▶ Trust them and give them responsibility to respond to various challenges.

▶ Be fair in your treatment.

▶ Facilitate creativity among your staff.

▶ Share all information with all your staff.

Learning to motivate is all about your own conviction in your staff's performance. Employees are motivated if they feel you do value them by giving them an opportunity to develop and to perform effectively.

Matching organisational goals with employees' aspirations is one of the key factors affecting motivation. (See opposite).

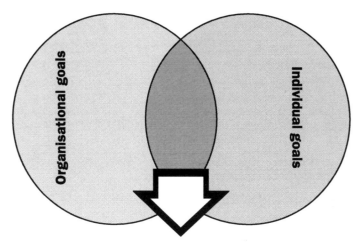

The more overlap, the better the motivation and performance

It is very important at recruitment stage to ascertain a candidate's short and long-term aspirations.

### Delegation v. empowerment

Delegation means assigning specific tasks to be performed by other people. The scope of responsibility and decision-making is limited and very often such a practice takes place within the hierarchical organisation.

### How to delegate

▶ Consider the tasks and associated 'responsibilities' you wish to delegate.

▶ Analyse the responsibility in terms of separate tasks and write these down.

▶ Write down which of these tasks can be delegated and which have to be done by you.

▶ List those tasks which have to be done by you and decide their order of priority.

▶ Set a timetable for yourself for completion of your tasks.

▶ List the individuals to whom you could delegate tasks.

▶ Rate their suitability for carrying out some or all of the tasks in terms of (a) capability and experience (b) availability (c) motivation and (d) other factors which may affect performance.

▶ Select the right candidate.

▶ Delegate work by explaining details and exercising 'active listening' to make sure that facts are clearly understood. Set a timescale and arrange time for checking progress, if necessary.

## ANALYSIS TOOL · DELEGATION

**The delegation continuum – beware of abdication!**

Do it and don't tell me about it.(Almost abdication.)

Do it and give me regular feedback.

Do it but wait for me to review it before you make any decision.

Draft it/wait for me to edit.

Outline it/wait for me to add input.

Only think about it. Give me suggestions.

Don't even think about it. Let us think aloud together.

## TOOL BOX 34THIRTY-FOUR

**What to delegate**

1. Responsibilities from a previous job that have no direct relation to your current managerial function.

2. Recurring routine detail

3. Routine decision-making.

4. Jobs that regularly consume large chunks of your time – certain reports, meetings, entertainments.

5. Jobs you are least qualified to handle.

6. Tasks that tend to under-specialise you, if your aim is to narrow your duties and concentrate in a desired technical field.

# What are the barriers to delegation in practice?

- Understaffed and overworked subordinates.

- Envy of subordinate ability.

- Insecurity.

- You the manager can do the job better and faster than your subordinates.

- Inability to explain the job clearly.

- Manager's lack of understanding of the task at hand.

- Manager being more comfortable 'doing' than 'managing'.

- Lack of organisational skill and balancing workloads.

- Inability to establish control.

- Failure to follow-up.

# Empowerment – power to your people

Empowerment has become a buzzword in the 1990s. Empowerment is presented as one of the key factors of motivation. It is an act of releasing human energy within an organisation. It is about giving authority and power to your people and trusting them to make decisions to solve problems. Organisations empower their people to achieve speed, flexibility and quality. Empowerment normally takes place in an organisation where there is no hierarchy or there are very few layers of organisation.

Researchers have shown that empowerment improves performance and employee effectiveness. It is, therefore, one of the key motivating factors.

### How to empower your people

▶ Share information on strategy and strategic objectives freely.

▶ Share information about the importance of changing environment.

▶ Share information about the importance of meeting customers' needs.

▶ Clarify what is empowered employees have to achieve.

▶ Set parameters of decision-making.

▶ Train staff to make decisions.

▶ Reward on performance.

▶ Provide encouragement and support to change.

▶ Change culture to tolerate mistakes.

If organisations do not empower their people they will not be able to recruit and retain people who can help them survive in a changing business climate.

## Motivation and performance

Giving people responsibility and power to make decisions help to motivate them. In order to sustain motivation, employees would like to know how they are performing, and feedback on their performance makes them feel they are valued. This feedback has to be structured and unbiased.

Many organisations have rituals of staff performance appraisals. Appraisals take place every three months or six months or once a year. Objectives which are set very often are not linked to strategic objectives and some managers find appraising their staff a chore.

Often appraisal interviews become acrimonious and not enough thought is given to preparation for such an important occasion.

If people are your most important asset then treat them as such and show them that you mean what you say. Their performance will reflect their competencies and organisational capabilities.

# How should you measure your staff performance?

**Measuring your staff performance**

1.  Provide your staff with information on your organisation's strategic objectives and your department's or team objectives.

2.  Explain the consistency between these sets of objectives.

3.  Inform your staff what is expected of them, why it is expected, how they contribute to the organisation's performance, how they should perform, by when they should be performed and how the results are going to be measured.

4.  Discuss the information given in 3 above to promote understanding and to take on board your staff's views.

5.  Ask your staff to tell you in writing what they currently do, what tasks and activities are involved, how they do their job and what roadblocks they face in performing their job.

6.  Match the information given by your staff to the information you have given to them.

7.  Help your staff set objectives for a given period, what and when outcomes are expected, and how they are going to be measured. Get an agreement.

## Measuring your staff performance

8. Prepare a measurement scale and explain it to your staff.

9. Now that your staff know what is expected and why, ask them to assess themselves on the scale you have agreed before an appraisal interview.

10. Do your preparation before the interview and have all the information you require ready and handy.

11. Treat your staff with respect and with courtesy.

12. Discuss the performance rating and indicate to what extent you agree with their assessment.

13. Whether you agree or disagree, do give your feedback.

14. Identify performance gaps and do discuss what should be done to fill these gaps and set the timescale.

15. Do use performance information to prepare a development plan of your staff and discuss this plan with them.

16. Explain the reward system and how it is linked to performance level.

17. Make performance appraisal interviews a pleasurable experience – something for your staff to look forward to in order to feel they are valued.

Performance appraisals should be undertaken quarterly or at least twice a year.

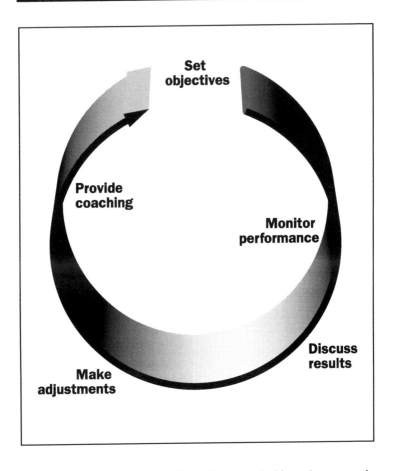

Performance, once measured has to be rewarded in order to sustain motivation. The reward system should be made clear to employees at the beginning. Reward should be fair, effective and satisfy needs.

# Coaching

The performance of staff contributes to overall performance of organisation. There has to be an element of continuous development as far as staff are concerned hence coaching plays a very crucial role in staff development, learning and motivation. Coaching is a technique of conditioning and shaping behaviour.

## Coaching involves:

1. explaining the drivers behind performance
2. talking through the stages of how to do it
3. watching how work is done
4. giving feedback
5. encouraging improved performance.

The main objective of coaching is to keep a trainee on the right track and to enhance effective performance. Coaching is related to performance appraisal. In the monitoring stage, a manager or a team leader has to coach in order to influence the performance of a team or departmental member.

Good leaders must also be a good coach. They must encourage certain behaviour and they must show by example. Coaching should be done on a continuous basis. Every contact you have with your staff provides you with coaching opportunity.

Coaching also involves providing a learning opportunity for your staff. Give your staff an opportunity to run a meeting, to make a decision, to conduct a discussion session, to make presentation. Give them feedback as to their performance and get them to improve their skills.

Modern day business demands a culture of constant and continuous improvement. According to Tom Peters, continuous improvement's baggage includes perpetual training, teamwork, risk-taking (by every one) continuous recognition, full-time listening, coaching rather than brow beating and scrapping the traditional adversarial ways the organisation deals with outsiders.

Many organisations do not believe in coaching. They would prefer to get their staff to 'hit the ground running' and take the responsibility of earning new skills themselves. This is a very short-sighted view. Development in people is an appreciating asset. If people really matter in your organisation then people development should be part of your business strategy.

## Coaching skill requires:

- good communication skills
- patience
- knowing how to give feedback
- delegation
- tolerance
- skill to ask rather than tell.

# Team building

Charles Handy in his book *Understanding Organisations* suggests ten major purposes for which organisations use groups or teams.

1. To bring together sets of skills or talents with a view to distributing work.

2. To manage and control work.

3. For problem-solving and decision-making.

4. For processing information.

5. For getting ideas and information.

6. For testing decisions.

7. For co-ordination and liaison.

8. For increased commitment and involvement.

9. For negotiation and conflict resolution.

10. For investigation.

## Attributes of a team

- There is trust among members.

- There is common purpose and vision.

- Sacrifices in individuality are demanded.

- There is discipline, guidance and associated performance indicators.

- There is group accountability.

- There is sharing of experience, knowledge and communication.

- There is commitment and involvement.

These attributes give rise to a spirit of 'teaming'. Teams per se are not important; it is the relationship and dynamics within the teams that matter.

# Team effectiveness

Teams effectiveness depends on structure, tasks, environment and process.

## Structure

**The size and composition of teams.** The bigger the team, the less effective it will be because it will be difficult to establish interpersonal relationships.

**Multi-skilled teams and their purpose.** What type of team members you want and why?

**Formation dynamics.** You have allowed time for team members to gel together.

## Tasks

**Identify nature of the task.** What is it you want your team to do?

*Objectives*
**Strategic alignment.** Are team objectives consistent with strategic objectives?

**Direction/coaching.** What type of direction and who is going to be a coach and a counsellor?

## Environment

**Structure.** How is your team going to be structured?

**Style.** What type of communication it is going to have?

**Systems.** What systems are put in place for your team to function properly?

**Empowerment**. How you are going to empower and what parameters are you going to establish?

## Process

Forming, storming, norming and performing. You have to allow your team to go through various processes to come into existence.

## Team building – cultural dimensions

*'Culture is like gravity; you do not experience it until you jump six feet into the air.'* **Fons Trompenaars**

It is important to consider prejudices, stereotyping, differences in values, attitudes and experiences in forming multi-cultural multi-skilled teams.

## Are you a good team player?

| Answer 'agree' or 'disagree' as appropriate | Agree | Disagree |
|---|---|---|
| 1. I am competent and a caring person. | ☐ | ☐ |
| 2. I like to communicate my ideas freely. | ☐ | ☐ |
| 3. I seldom question the usefulness of any decision. | ☐ | ☐ |
| 4. I go along with what others say or do. | ☐ | ☐ |
| 5. I do not like to say what I really think. | ☐ | ☐ |
| 6. I trust my leader. | ☐ | ☐ |
| 7. I do not trust team members. | ☐ | ☐ |
| 8. I like working in a team because I do not like making decisions. | ☐ | ☐ |
| 9. I do not like to be criticised. | ☐ | ☐ |
| 10. Teams are a nice way of fudging business problems. | ☐ | ☐ |
| 11. I do not like to express views on my colleagues' performance. | ☐ | ☐ |
| 12. I do not feel strengthened by my colleagues. | ☐ | ☐ |
| 13. I like to question the way we operate. | ☐ | ☐ |
| 14. I believe in tighter supervision. | ☐ | ☐ |
| 15. Working in a team is a waste of time. | ☐ | ☐ |
| 16. I like to defend my expertise when I am in a team. | ☐ | ☐ |
| 17. I make an attempt to understand the views of others. | ☐ | ☐ |
| 18. I like to be consulted. | ☐ | ☐ |
| 19. I am not prepared to express what I believe in openly. | ☐ | ☐ |

## Are you a good team player?

| Answer 'agree' or 'disagree' as appropriate | Agree | Disagree |
|---|:---:|:---:|
| 20. I do not like raising delicate issues. | ☐ | ☐ |
| 21. I like thinking new ideas. | ☐ | ☐ |
| 22. I am ready to be unpopular if I can improve the situation. | ☐ | ☐ |
| 23. I like people to listen to me all the time. | ☐ | ☐ |
| 24. I am responsive to the needs of my team. | ☐ | ☐ |
| 25. I have an aptitude of influencing others. | ☐ | ☐ |
| 26. I get very angry and frustrated if I do not get my way. | ☐ | ☐ |
| 27. I like working with others. | ☐ | ☐ |
| 28. I work better on my own. | ☐ | ☐ |
| 29. I am not good at getting my points across. | ☐ | ☐ |
| 30. I get bored very easily in a team situation. | ☐ | ☐ |

## Scoring

Give *one* point if you **agree** or *two* points if you **disagree** to 1, 2, 6, 13, 17, 18, 21, 22, 25, 27.

Give *two* points if you **agree** and *one* point if you **disagree** to 3, 4, 5, 7, 8, 9, 10, 11, 12, 14, 15, 16, 19, 20, 23, 24, 26, 28, 29, 30.

| | |
|---|---|
| **30-32** points | You are a very good team player. |
| **33-36** points | You are still good but you can improve. |
| **37-45** points | You have to work very hard to fit in a team. |
| **46+** points | I am glad you are not in my team. you are definitely not a team player. |

© Sultan Kermally

# CHAPTER 12TWELVE

# Communication

# Communication

**ALMOST EVERY PROBLEM** in any organisation can be blamed on lack of communication or poor communication. Top managers fail to communicate corporate strategy clearly and openly. As a result workers do not perform effectively and as a result business objectives are not fully achieved. In some cases workers' morale becomes very low because they feel they do not know what is happening in their organisations.

Information is not communication. Communication by its very nature is a two-way traffic. Information has to be assimilated and feedback has to be forthcoming.

## Poor communication occurs due to

a) use of jargon

b) an individual sifts information depending on their attitude, mood etc

c) the message is deliberately distorted

d) overloading of information

e) lack of structure to facilitate communication

f) values and perceptions of recipients

g) differences in culture.

Whether in providing effective leadership or in motivating your staff it is important to promote honest and open communication. Joseph Luft and Harry Ingham developed a framework which is known as Johari Window. (See opposite.)

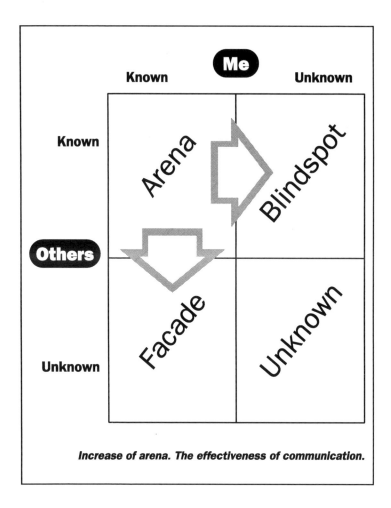

*Increase of arena. The effectiveness of communication.*

According to this framework there is information which is known to yourself and there is some information which is not known to yourself. In dealing with other parts (individuals, groups, organisations), there is information known to them and not known to them.

Information which is known to you and others is in **public** domain (**Arena**).

Information which is known to you but not others is in **private** domain (**Facade**). Information which is known to others but not to you is in a **blind** area and information which is not known to you and not known to others is in an **unknown** domain.

In order to enhance organisational performance, and to promote open and honest communication, employees as well as those who fall into the 'others' category (top managers, leaders, senior managers) should make an attempt to widen the **public** domain arena. When information flows freely from you to others, this is the process known as **feedback**. When information flows freely from 'others' to you, this process is known as **disclosure**.

In promoting effective leadership and in motivating staff it is important to enhance the process of feedback and disclosure.

---

### TOOL BOX 37 THIRTY-SEVEN

#### Promoting effective communication

▶ Select words carefully.

▶ Establish effective channels of communication.

▶ Make each manager responsible for effective communication in their area.

▶ Ask for feedback.

▶ Listen very carefully.

▶ Interpret and evaluate feedback.

▶ Empathise with your staff.

▶ Reflect enthusiasm in relation to the subject matter of communication.

---

We use communication all the time to give information, to send messages, to provide instruction, to express our feelings and emotions, to negotiate and to express our opinions about other people. Communication is not just about what you say but how you say it.

## Communicating assertively

To be assertive is to have concern for yourself and concern for others. It is about expressing your feelings and views openly and honestly without hurting others. Not having concern for other people leads to aggression. See below.

**ANALYSIS TOOL · CONCERN FOR SELF AND OTHERS**

|  |  | Concern for self | |
|---|---|---|---|
|  |  | High | Low |
| **Concern for others** | High | Assertiveness | Potentially stressful |
|  | Low | Aggressiveness Selfish | Passive behaviour |

There are various techniques used in practice to become assertive. Some of these techniques are incorporated in Tool box 38 (overleaf).

### Becoming assertive

1. Express your feelings and views openly and calmly.

2. Explain the reasons behind your feelings, views and opinions.

3. When you are not sure what you are expected to do ask for explanation or clarification.

4. Do not bottle up your feelings.

5. If you are asked to do something and you have no time seek information on priority.

6. Learn to say 'no' effectively and explain why you say 'no'.

7. If you are receiving mixed messages do ask for clarification.

8. Listen very carefully to what others say.

9. Explain clearly what you want to happen

10. Use 'however' when you need to use 'but'. 'I know you want this done immediately, however...' 'However' has positive impact on the listener.

11. Always look for a win-win situation. Come up with compromises.

12. Control your anger and teach yourself to think positively.

13. Do sympathise with the other party but be firm in what you want to say or do.

The above points are very simple and straightforward but you need to practice them to form a habit of communicating assertively.

# Making presentations

There are three key components (three Ss) of making effective presentations. They are:

1. **Strategy**: Involving planning, determining objectives, analysing audience, event and location.

2. **Substance**: The message you want to convey.

3. **Style**: Involving voice, pacing, tone, gestures and posture.

In other words, it is important to consider what you want to say, why you want to say it, to whom you want to say it and how you want to say it.

## The 'Tell 'Em' principle

- Tell them what you are going to say.
- Then tell them.
- Tell them what you have said.

## Opening

**What is the theme?**

## Delivery

**Concise and clear**. Give examples and relate to the audience.

## Summary

**Reinforce key points you have made**. Leave no room for doubt about your message.

The image one projects by appearance, words, delivery and personality greatly influences three things:

- the way in which audiences respond
- the degree of influence of the message and
- the extent to which the message is assimilated.

---

**TOOL BOX 39 THIRTY-NINE**

### How to make a successful presentation

▶ Prepare. Be familiar with your material.

▶ Rehearse. This is important.

▶ Walk confidently to the lectern. Do not use it as your psychological crutch.

▶ Arrange your notes.

▶ Establish eye contact with your audience.

▶ Resist the temptation to speak fast.

▶ Pace your voice. Change your pitch and volume.

▶ Speak clearly.

---

# Negotiating successfully

Negotiation is a process of arriving at mutual satisfaction through exchange of information. Negotiation takes place at home among family members, at work among colleagues and with senior managers and with other individuals and groups outside your organisation. The important thing about negotiation is not to adopt a 'macho' attitude but to go through the process with a **win-win** attitude. Winning a negotiation at the expense of the other party may be a losing proposition in the long run.

To go with a positive attitude you have to be:

- honest
- have consideration for other party involved in negotiation
- careful not top adopt confrontational attitude
- listen carefully
- careful not to expose weaknesses of the other party.

The outcome of any negotiation depends on the issues involved and how strong you feel about them. In some cases issues do not matter very much. What may be crucial will be creating and sustaining a good relationship with the party with whom you are negotiating.

---

**TOOL BOX 40FORTY**

**Managing the negotiation process**

Before you go through negotiating process consider the following:

▶ What outcome do you desire?

▶ What would the other party want the outcome to be?

▶ How big is the gap?

▶ How are you going to reduce this gap?

▶ What trade-off are you are prepared to make?

▶ What is your last resort trade-off?

▶ What kind of knowledge and power do you need to have at the negotiation?

▶ Have you done enough preparation?

▶ What is the time pressure?

▶ What happens if you do not get your desired outcome?

---

## Techniques to help you negotiate successfully

1.  Do establish 'rapport' with the other party. Reflect your positive attitude and at the outset state that you are after a win-win situation. Come prepared with some conversation openers.

2.  During the process of negotiation do ask open questions to explore statements being made. Do listen very carefully at what is being said and do observe body language and the tone of the communication.

3.  When making your offer do explain the reasons behind the offer.

    Do indicate that this is not a 'take or leave it' offer. If the other party makes an offer ask for explanation and do ask closed questions to make sure you understand the offer being made.

4.  Propose trade-off and make concessions gracefully without implying any weakness.

    Do come to some resolution. At the end of the day if you have to disagree, do so without being disagreeable.

5.  If you arrive at deadlocks, focus on the problem. Limit the scope of the problem and do take a break to rethink the situation.

6.  Focus on the area of agreement and do come to mutually satisfactory conclusions in certain aspects of your negotiation.

# CHAPTER 13THIRTEEN

## Managing change

# Managing change

**CHANGE IS INEVITABLE** in many organisations these days. Organisations operate within the context of external environments. External environments involve sociological, technological, economic and political factors. These factors impact upon every organisation. At present, uncertainty and financial chaos in many Asian economies affect businesses in the countries outside Asia. The single currency will impact upon the transaction costs of many businesses. Technological developments will increasingly reduce the labour force and create more redundancies.

In addition, international markets are opening up and new competitors are appearing from every direction. The marketplace is changing into market space and customers are becoming more demanding and discriminatory.

All these factors mean that businesses have to change in order to compete effectively.

It was stated in chapters one and two that businesses are affected by external as well as internal factors. What happens within the industry sector impacts the strategy of a business. By conducting an impact analysis one can assess the changes taking place externally and by undertaking industry analysis along the lines suggested by Michael Porter one can assess the changes taking place internally. The two sets of factors, external and internal, are interdependent.

## What is needed for bringing about change?

1. Commitment from top management. Without such commitment the change process will fade away very quickly.

2. There needs to be a clear vision of the future and business direction.

3. Vision and direction has to be communicated to all employees and the communication has to be simple, clear and open.

4. Explain why there is a need to bring about change and what will happen if nothing is done.

5. All employees should be involved in the change process and they should be clear about the role they can play.

6. Systems and procedures and teams have to be put in place to bring about desired change.

7. There should be a proper assessment of resources required and these resources should be allocated accordingly.

8. Any change will bring about uncertainty and some instability. Do manage the human side of change properly.

## Method of managing change

The most common method was introduced by Kurt Lewin, a psychologist. He suggested that we can look at any organisation or any situation as being held in balance, or equilibrium, between two forces. These are forces which are driving it and forces which are restraining it. In a stable situation the forces balance each other out. This method is known as **Force – Field Analysis**.

## The driving forces

The driving forces could be sociological factors, technological factors, economic factors, political factors, ideological factors, cultural factors, competition and competitors, customers' needs, effective leadership, capabilities and competencies.

These are the factors that drive change forward and enable organisations to meet their objectives.

## The restraining factors

The restraining factors hold back change and cause friction. These factors are cultural factors; personal attitude; weak leadership; poor communication; fear of unknown; structure, systems and procedures; resources and capabilities.

**ANALYSIS TOOL · FORCE-FIELD ANALYSIS**

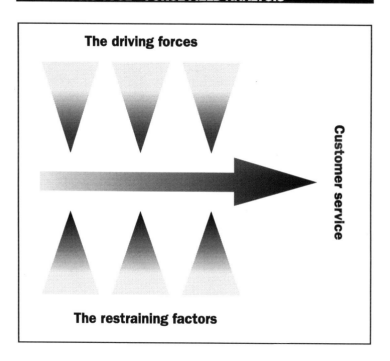

**The driving forces**

Customer service

**The restraining factors**

If you were to bring about a change in any part of your organisation what would be the driving forces? Indicate them on the **top** of the arrow. What would be the restraining forces? Indicate them at the **bottom** of the arrow.

In practice resistance to change occurs due to loss of power, poor communication, possibility of more work, uncertainty, loss of employment, loss of face, more hassles, concern about future competence and so on. It is very important to identify the sources and the causes of resistance.

**To overcome resistance requires a lot of thought, consideration, training, involvement, patience and participation.**

# CHAPTER 14FOURTEEN

# Re-engineering your business process

# Re-engineering your business processes

**MANY ORGANISATIONS IN** the past decade have embarked upon re-engineering their business processes in order to improve their operational efficiency and to get close to the customers. Michael Hammer and James Champy published a book entitled *Re-engineering the Corporation* (1993) in which they advocated the radical reinvention of the way work is done in many organisation. As the message was focused mainly for American companies they wrote 'To reinvent their companies, American managers must throw out their old notions about how businesses should be organised and run. They must abandon the organisational and operational principles and procedures they are now using and create entirely new rules.'

As with many new management ideas, the practice spread to Europe, and many organisations, private and public, decided to re-engineer their business processes. Companies like AT&T, the National Provincial Building Society, National Health Service, Hall Mark, British Telecom and so on saw dramatic improvements in their operational efficiency as a result of process re-engineering.

## What is it?

It is simply a method of analysing all the processes involved in running any business. Analyse all activities involved in each process and ask a simple question. Does this activity in a specific process add value to the end result? Does this process add value to the end result? If the answer is no, eliminate it.

The focus is on processes. A process is defined as a set of linked activities that take an input and transform it to create an output.

## Preparing to re-engineer your business processes

▶ Keep all processes very simple.

▶ Integrate various tasks and activities into one and assign it to one person.

▶ Make sure that work is performed where it makes most sense.

▶ Reduce hierarchy and delayer your organisation.

▶ Rethink all the processes involved with the customer in mind.

▶ Use technology to integrate activities and processes.

▶ Align all core processes to your corporate strategy.

▶ Trust and empower your staff.

▶ Allow risk-taking and be tolerant to mistakes made.

▶ Challenge all existing assumptions on which your business is based.

▶ Train your staff.

**How to re-engineer** *(Start with a clean sheet of paper)*

*Step 1*

▶ Consider all the processes involved.

▶ Prepare process maps (mapping all the processes involved).

▶ Distinguish between core processes and support processes.

*Step 2*

▶ Focus your attention on core processes at first.

▶ Decide and plan how you are going to do it.

▶ Decide who is to do it.

▶ Decide on the timescale involved.

▶ Decide which measurement indicators will be used to monitor progress.

*Step 3*

▶ Form a project team.

▶ Appoint a project manager.

▶ Make sure the team is interdisciplinary.

*Step 4*

▶ Start the project.

▶ Communicate objectives to all involved.

▶ Allocate various tasks to project team members.

▶ Establish parameters and the method of monitoring.

▶ Keep open and full communication going all the time.

Success of business re-engineering will depend ultimately on how well you have planned it, how competent are the people involved in implementing it and what you have provided.

# CHAPTER 15 FIFTEEN

# Managing stress

# Managing stress

> 'He who knows others is clever.
>
> He who knows himself is wiser.' **Source: Unknown**

**CHANGES IN AN** organisation create stress for some employees. It is very important nowadays to understand the nature of stress.

It has been estimated that between 50 and 75 per cent of health problems are either caused by stress or significantly exacerbated by it. Stress affects our life expectancy, our creativity, our judgement, our tendency to make mistakes and our proneness to accidents.

## Pressure v. stress

Some experts say that some stress is good for you, they classify stress as having a negative effect as well as a positive effect. This in my view is a mistake. Stress always has a negative effect and should be avoided. What is positive and useful is pressure. Some people perform better when they have pressure put on them. However, when this pressure becomes too much because of lack of time or ability or resources then the situation turns into a stressful situation.

The threshold between pressure and stress varies from person to person. It depends on personality, culture, the type of pressure involved, personal circumstances and so on. Threshold also varies within each individual.

Situations which cause stress are:

- death
- marital problems
- divorce
- financial problems
- illness
- discrimination
- bullying
- unemployment
- interpersonal conflict
- unhappiness: work/personal.

When we are in stressful situations, adrenaline is pumped round the body, the heart rate increases, blood pressure rises, our muscles become tense, and our breathing quickens.

# What are the symptoms?

The symptoms can be broken down into three categories.

### Physiological symptoms

- High blood pressure.
- Increased heart beat.
- Dryness of throat and mouth.
- Increased sweating. Nausea.

## Psychological symptoms

- Irritability.
- Anxiety.
- Frustration.
- Anger.
- Fatigue.
- Migraines.
- Lack of confidence.
- Insomnia.

## Behavioural symptoms

- Addiction.
- Inability to concentrate.
- Impulsive behaviour.
- Feeling of being keyed up.

The above list is not exhaustive.

Stress is a situation caused by imbalance. This is an imbalance between our efforts and perceived results. It is our perception of consequences which create stress in us. If you feel you are never on top of your job, or you do not have skills to perform what is expected of you or you cannot give any more time to finish tasks allocated to you, you start perceiving negative consequences which in turn create stress. It is our perception of events (consequences) rather than the events themselves which is the problem.

## TOOL BOX 45 FORTY-FIVE

### How to cope with stress

▶ Think positive. You are what you think.

▶ Examine what type of a person you are. What are your strengths and weaknesses.

▶ Pay attention to your weaknesses.

▶ Discuss your problems with your boss, colleagues, family members or friends.

▶ Review your priorities regularly.

▶ Plan your time effectively.

▶ Identify your 'stressors' and think what you can do to minimise or eliminate them.

▶ Watch your diet.

▶ Do regular exercise.

The following is a questionnaire prepared by Dr. Jagdish Parikh, the author of *Managing Self*.

|     |                                                      | Yes | Sometimes | No |
|-----|------------------------------------------------------|-----|-----------|----|
| **1.**  | I eat at least one hot meal a day.               | 1   | 2         | 3  |
| **2.**  | I do smoke.                                       | 1   | 2         | 3  |
| **3.**  | I do take alcoholic drinks.                       | 1   | 2         | 3  |
| **4.**  | I exercise regularly.                             | 1   | 2         | 3  |
| **5.**  | I am overweight.                                  | 1   | 2         | 3  |
| **6.**  | I get good sleep at least five nights a week.     | 1   | 2         | 3  |
| **7.**  | I do lose my temper most of the time.             | 1   | 2         | 3  |
| **8.**  | I am very tolerant to other people's views.       | 1   | 2         | 3  |
| **9.**  | I am aggressive most of the time.                 | 1   | 2         | 3  |
| **10.** | I am very passive most of the time.               | 1   | 2         | 3  |
| **11.** | I often feel depressed.                           | 1   | 2         | 3  |
| **12.** | I have someone to confide in about my personal matters. | 1 | 2     | 3  |
| **13.** | I find it difficult to concentrate on things I do. | 1  | 2         | 3  |
| **14.** | I am able to speak openly and frankly.            | 1   | 2         | 3  |
| **15.** | I do push myself when I am tired.                 | 1   | 2         | 3  |
| **16.** | I feel confident in all the things I do.          | 1   | 2         | 3  |

## How vulnerable are you to stress?

|  | Yes | Sometimes | No |
|---|---|---|---|
| **17**. I manage my time properly. | 1 | 2 | 3 |
| **18**. I plan my day. | 1 | 2 | 3 |
| **19**. I do have objectives for personal goals. | 1 | 2 | 3 |
| **20**. I have adequate income for my basic needs. | 1 | 2 | 3 |
| **21**. I can stand criticisms. | 1 | 2 | 3 |
| **22**. I meditate once a day. | 1 | 2 | 3 |
| **23**. I take a quiet time for myself during the day. | 1 | 2 | 3 |
| **24**. I get comfort from my religious beliefs. | 1 | 2 | 3 |

### Scoring

Score points as indicated under Yes, Sometimes and No.

Add up your figure and subtract 24.

| | |
|---|---|
| 0-6 | You can manage your stress very effectively. |
| 7-18 | You need to pay attention to your stress level. |
| 19-38 | You are vulnerable to stress. |
| 39+ | You are very vulnerable to stress. |

© Jagdish Parikh

# CHAPTER 16SIXTEEN

# Corporate culture

# Corporate culture

**CORPORATE CULTURE SHOULD** be of interest to every organisation – large or small. It is the culture of an organisation that creates effective leadership and brings about changes in the organisation to make it flexible to meet the demands of customers. Culture is not an 'airy fairy' thing of interest only to sociologists.

## What is corporate culture?

Culture in an organisation is the complex body of shared values and beliefs. In forming corporate strategy, organisations have to consider the environment within which they operate and they also have to consider how to adapt to a changing environment. They formulate strategy to cope with the changing situation and to achieve their desired objectives. The way these objectives are achieved is underpinned by the beliefs and values the organisation holds. These beliefs and values direct behaviour of all those working in the organisation. Culture, therefore, becomes 'the way we do things in our organisation'.

Culture provides the glue to hold organisation members together. When you join any organisation you hear stories about past characters, about present leaders, you get information about the dress code, about behaviour expected. All these constitute corporate culture.

# What is the role of culture?

- It provides a sense of identity.

- It directs behaviour.

- It generates commitment to values.

- It provides corporate cohesion.

- It reflects the vision and strategy of an organisation.

- It guides day-to-day relationships among members.

- It influences how power and status is allocated.

- It determines the way we respond to customers and other stake-holders. Corporate culture is reflected by the use of symbols and ceremonies.

- It affects the way people are promoted in an organisation.

- It affects the way performance is measured.

- It affects the way employees are rewarded.

Corporate culture, therefore, affects the entire operation of any business.

Culture in an organisation can be categorised as :

- **Adaptive culture** which facilitate changes to meet external and internal demands.

- **Collaborative culture** which promotes the feeling of togetherness in an organisation.

- **Co-existence culture** which encourages diversity in an organisation.

- **Tolerant culture** which allows for mistakes in order to promote staff development.

- **Clan culture** where there is commitment to corporate values.

- **Bureaucratic culture** where behaviour and actions are controlled by procedures and policies.

Even though we talk about *one* corporate culture, in practice an organisation is *multi*-culture entity. Different departments, different specialities and different teams will develop their norms and values and bring about subcultures within an organisation. If these subcultures are in clash with one another or with corporate culture then there will be conflict and there will be many unhappy employees. there will be a group of people acting as 'silent sabotage'. They will moan about and criticise the company at any opportunity that comes their way.

When companies go through various changes – when they downsize or introduce a total quality initiative or when they re-engineer their processes or when they introduce empowerment – such initiatives impact upon corporate culture as well subcultures.

---

**ANALYSIS TOOL**

### What kind of culture is in your organisation?

- Service culture.
- Culture of respect.
- Culture of trust.
- Tolerant culture.
- Adaptive culture.
- Culture of open communication.
- Culture of collaboration.
- 'Dog eat dog' culture.
- Culture of recognition of employees.
- Culture of '*who* you know rather than *what* you know'.

---

'The way we do things over here' impacts upon the behaviour and performance of all employees and subsequently the performance of an organisation as a whole. A culture which is strong in its values but flexible enough to facilitate adaptation is desirable to survive in a competitive world.

## Is your organisation effective?

*Scoring*

1. Totally agree.

2. I tend to agree.

3. I do not know.

4. I tend to disagree.

5. I totally disagree.

### Corporate perspective

**1.** Our organisation has a mission statement.

   1     2     3     4     5

**2.** Everyone or most employees know our organisation's mission statement.

   1     2     3     4     5

**3.** Our strategy/strategic objectives are communicated to all employees.

   1     2     3     4     5

**4.** Our strategic planning involves all departments/division/team heads.

   1     2     3     4     5

**5.** Our organisation's mission statement is very clearly expressed.

   1     2     3     4     5

**6.** All departments in our organisation have clear and specific objectives.

   1     2     3     4     5

## Is your organisation effective?

*Scoring*

1. Totally agree.
2. I tend to agree.
3. I do not know.
4. I tend to disagree.
5. I totally disagree.

**7.** All/ most employees have great respect for our chief executive officer/managing director.

   1      2      3      4      5

**8.** We have free access to information on our organisation by approaching appropriate individuals/departments.

   1      2      3      4      5

**9.** Our organisation undertakes an analysis of its external environment.

   1      2      3      4      5

**10.** All departments/divisions/teams are expected to make a contribution to external environment analysis.

   1      2      3      4      5

**11.** All jobs in our organisation are clearly defined.

   1      2      3      4      5

**12.** There is good communication in our organisation between departments/sections/teams.

   1      2      3      4      5

**13.** Our chief executive officer/managing director is a 'visible' figure in our organisation.

   1      2      3      4      5

**14.** We do trust our chief executive officer/managing director.

1     2     3     4     5

**15.** We are kept informed of our organisation's performance on a regular basis.

1     2     3     4     5

**16.** All/most employees are highly committed to the strategic goals of our organisation.

1     2     3     4     5

**17.** We/most of us are very proud to work for our organisation.

1     2     3     4     5

**18.** Our organisation values its people.

1     2     3     4     5

**19.** Our organisation recognises people for doing good work.

1     2     3     4     5

**20.** We are encouraged to express our views on management and performance in relation to our organisation.

1     2     3     4     5

**21.** Our strategy incorporates meeting customers' satisfaction.

1     2     3     4     5

**22.** Our chief executive/managing director visits some of our customers.

1     2     3     4     5

**23.** Our organisation tries to align customer satisfaction with employee satisfaction.

1     2     3     4     5

**24**. Our company believes in staff training.

    1        2        3        4        5

**25**. Our company spends a proportion of its revenue on staff training.

    1        2        3        4        5

**26**. Before undertaking staff training our organisation does training needs analysis.

    1        2        3        4        5

**27**. In assessing training needs all employees are consulted.

    1        2        3        4        5

**28**. Our organisation keeps in close contact with some of our key customers.

    1        2        3        4        5

**29**. Our organisations keep in close contact with our suppliers.

    1        2        3        4        5

**30**. Our organisation considers our suppliers as partners.

    1        2        3        4        5

**31**. Our organisation reviews the process of delivering customer service.

    1        2        3        4        5

**32**. Our organisation reviews the process of product/service management.

    1        2        3        4        5

**33**. Our organisation encourages creativity among staff.

    1        2        3        4        5

**34.** Inside our organisation we treat each other as customers.

    1        2        3        4        5

**35.** If we hear any bad comments about our organisation we do tell our boss.

    1        2        3        4        5

**36.** Our organisation does not pay too much attention to what city analysts write or to its shareholders.

    1        2        3        4        5

**37.** Our organisation considers the interests of direct stakeholders.

    1        2        3        4        5

**38.** Our organisation does listen to its customers.

    1        2        3        4        5

**39.** Customers are included in our mission statement.

    1        2        3        4        5

**40.** In our organisation we are all concerned with delivering quality.

    1        2        3        4        5

## Is your organisation effective?

*Scoring*

1. Totally agree.
2. I tend to agree.
3. I do not know.
4. I tend to disagree.
5. I totally disagree.

### Operational perspective

**1.** My manager/supervisor/team leader sets performance goals for us.

    1     2     3     4     5

**2.** We work as a team in our department.

    1     2     3     4     5

**3.** We communicate with one another in our department.

    1     2     3     4     5

**4.** We get good support from our manager/supervisor/ team leader.

    1     2     3     4     5

**5.** Mistakes are tolerated in our department.

    1     2     3     4     5

**6.** Our manager/supervisor/team leader is very approachable.

    1     2     3     4     5

**7.** Our manager/supervisor/team leader keep us informed of the progress of our department.

    1     2     3     4     5

**8.** We can always rely on getting help from our manager/supervisor/team leader.

    1       2       3       4       5

**9.** In our department we help each other, when necessary.

    1       2       3       4       5

**10.** We do have clear information on what we are expected to do.

    1       2       3       4       5

**11.** We do have clear performance goals in our department.

    1       2       3       4       5

**12.** We are involved in setting our own performance goals.

    1       2       3       4       5

**13.** Our individual/team performance goals are linked with the organisation's overall goals.

    1       2       3       4       5

**14.** Our goals are monitored every three/six months.

    1       2       3       4       5

**15.** We do have performance appraisals every three/six months.

    1       2       3       4       5

**16.** We are given time to prepare for our appraisals.

    1       2       3       4       5

**17.** We do know exactly what our standards of performance should be.

    1       2       3       4       5

## Is your organisation effective?

*Scoring*

1. Totally agree.

2. I tend to agree.

3. I do not know.

4. I tend to disagree.

5. I totally disagree.

**18.** We do look forward to our performance appraisals.

    1      2      3      4      5

**19.** We are given information on our strengths and weaknesses at our appraisals.

    1      2      3      4      5

**20.** Our appraisals are used to develop our training programmes.

    1      2      3      4      5

**21.** We get very good feedback from our appraisals.

    1      2      3      4      5

**22.** Our manager/supervisor/team leader is very good at giving positive and constructive feedback after appraisals.

    1      2      3      4      5

**23.** We do get feedback within a month of our appraisals.

    1      2      3      4      5

**24.** Our manager/supervisor/team leader gives us recognition for our good performance.

    1      2      3      4      5

**25**. Our manager/supervisor/team leader is very enthusiastic about the work.

    1        2        3        4        5

**26**. Our manager/supervisor/team leader is available to help us, when necessary.

    1        2        3        4        5

**27**. We do have clearly defined responsibilities in our department.

    1        2        3        4        5

**28**. We do have a regular meetings in our department.

    1        2        3        4        5

**29**. We find meetings in our department or organisation very useful.

    1        2        3        4        5

**30**. We do trust our manager/supervisor/team leader.

    1        2        3        4        5

## Is your organisation effective?

*Scoring*

1. Totally agree.

2. I tend to agree.

3. I do not know.

4. I tend to disagree.

5. I totally disagree.

### Personal perspective

**1.** I can manage my time properly.

   1     2     3     4     5

**2.** I do not work long hours.

   1     2     3     4     5

**3.** I do not find my work very stressful.

   1     2     3     4     5

**4.** I do not take work home very regularly.

   1     2     3     4     5

**5.** If I am stressed I can discuss my situation with my colleagues.

   1     2     3     4     5

**6.** I can approach my manager/supervisor/team leader if I have any problems.

   1     2     3     4     5

**7.** I can approach my manager/supervisor/team leader if I have good ideas for the department.

   1     2     3     4     5

**8.** My pay and prospects are linked to my performance.

    1      2      3      4      5

**9.** I like working for my department.

    1      2      3      4      5

**10.** I can get training in acquiring new skills if I ask for it.

    1      2      3      4      5

## Scoring

This questionnaire is divided into three sections, namely a corporate section, operational section and personal section.

The scoring scale is as follows:

| | | | |
|---|---|---|---|
| *I strongly agree.* | *1.* | *I tend to disagree.* | *4.* |
| *I tend to agree.* | *2.* | *I strongly disagree.* | *5.* |
| *I am not sure.* | *3.* | | |

*please turn over*

### Your score

*40 points*
*Excellent.* Your organisation is managed very well. It is well placed to undertake a balanced performance approach and to consider the needs of all stakeholders.

*41-50 points*
*Very good.* Your organisation is managed well but it can do better. It is well placed to undertake meaningful performance management.

*51-80 points*
*Good.* Your organisation is well placed to improve significantly and manage its performance effectively.

*81-100 points*
*Average.* Your organisation ,if not careful, will end up managed badly and lose its competitive strength.

*101-140 points*
*Bad.* Your organisation has an opportunity to improve significantly by paying attention to its strategy formulation and interests of all its direct stakeholders.

*141-180 points*
*Very bad.* Your organisation is very badly managed. It has a short-term survival prospect.

*181-200 points*
*Extremely bad.* Your organisation has total disregard for its people and other stakeholders. I am surprised it still exists.

*Note:* Many organisations work efficiently but not effectively. To be effective organisations have to work efficiently to achieve its corporate objectives. These objectives should embrace interests of shareholders and other stakeholders including customers and employees.

## OPERATIONAL PERSPECTIVE SCORING

*30 points*

*Excellent.* Your department is excellent. However, to be effective the score has to match a very low score at Organisational perspective.

*31-60 points*

*Very good.* Your department has very good potential of achieving excellent status. Again consistency with low score at organisational level is important.

*61-90 points*

*Good.* Your department scores average performance. It has potential to improve significantly.

*91-120 points*

*Bad.* Your department is managed badly. If it is achieving its desired results now then these results will not be sustained.

*120-150 points*

*Very bad.* The morale and the staff turnover of your department must be very bad.

*Note:* To be effective and sustain good results, departmental objectives and results must be consistent with organisational objectives. Low score at this section (up to 60 points) and high score at organisational level section (160 points) would suggest that the departmental and organisational performance are out of sync.

# On becoming a learning organisation

Developing staff by training, mentoring and coaching has become very important in many businesses today in order to gain and sustain competitive advantage. In a crisis situation many organisations feel the way to compete effectively is to reduce costs and to make employees redundant. This is only a very short-term solution. To compete effectively over a long period involves building new skills and responding to customer needs.

Peter Senge's book *The Fifth Discipline* (1995) popularised the concept of the learning organisation.

According to Senge the learning organisation has the capacity to be innovative and such an organisation continuously encourages the development of intellectual (thinking) as well as pragmatic (doing) dimensions.

## How to become a learning organisation

▶ Have a mission of your organisation.

▶ Encourage creativity and innovation.

▶ Encourage acquisition of knowledge and new skills.

▶ Develop core competencies in your organisation.

▶ Develop the culture of honest and open communication.

▶ Discard the attitude of 'if it ain't broke, don't fix it'.

▶ Recognise achievements.

▶ Provide resources to update skills.

▶ Monitor competition.

▶ Do benchmarking of best practice.

▶ Focus on customers.

▶ Empower your staff.

▶ Have courage to adapt your organisation's structure.

Learning is about development and change. Change is the norm in the world today.

# CHAPTER 17 SEVENTEEN

## 'Outside the box' thinking

# 'Outside the box' thinking

**THE IMPORTANT THING** in the business world today is not to work hard but to work smart. Working smart involves breaking out of our perceptions and looking for different possibilities.

## Mind gymnastics

We, as human beings, go through various processes to become aware of our environment. This process involves the selection of stimuli, organising them according to our experience and upbringing (socialisation process). These processes are not perfect. We do often mis-perceive and make judgements (see diagrams below).

*Paris in the the spring*

*A walk in in the park*

In asking someone to read them they would read 'Paris in the spring' and 'A walk in the park'. Very few people notice the second 'the' and the second 'in'.

Very often we face the same situation but arrive at different conclusions. Look at the picture below. What do you see?

Some people see a rabbit while some may see a duck or a sort of a bird. This is how perception affects our judgement.

Our perceptions also condition us to look at a particular problem in a certain way. Look below.

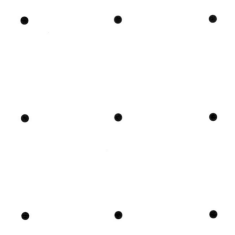

Join all nine dots with four lines without removing your pen or pencil. People who find it difficult do so because they are trying to join the dots within the square (they want to remain in a box). There is no rule that says we must do so within the context of a square. But because our mind perceives a square it forms a sort of a trap and it stops us from coming to a solution.

Once it is shown how to connect all nine dots, it becomes apparent that we have to break outside the square or a box. This is what thinking outside the box is all about.

If we are then given a second challenge of connecting 16 dots by using six lines, it is relatively easy to do so because our mind has been conditioned to think outside the box.

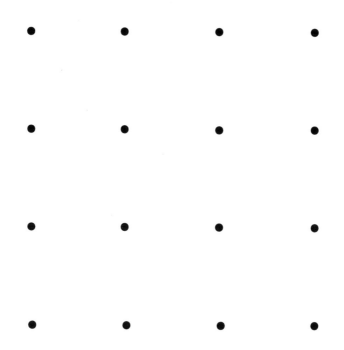

Thinking outside the box involves unlearning. It has been said that unlearning is more difficult than learning. According to Dennis Sherwood, the author of *Unblock your Mind*, there is always another way of doing things if only we can unlock our minds.

**Nine dot solution.**

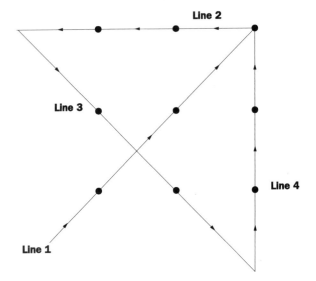

**Sixteen dot solution.**

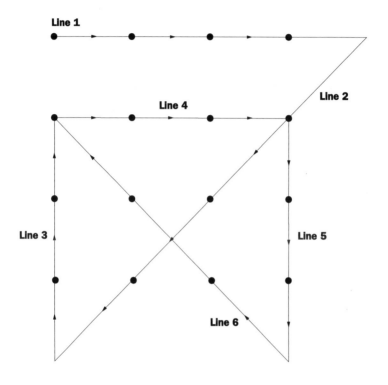

# READING TOOL BOX

## For busy managers

# Reading tool box

## Stay up-to-date on current management thinking

This section deals with suggestion on reading on the subjects covered in this book. There is very brief information on what each book or article covers.

Adams Scott. *The Dilbert Principle* (1996). Boxtree Ltd, UK.

ISBN 0 7522 2287 2

Light hearted approach to present day management. As the book cover says 'a cubicle's eye view of bosses, meetings, management fads and other workplace afflictions.'

Bennis Warren, Parikh Jagdis, Lessem Ronnie.
*Beyond Leadership* (1994). Basil Blackwell, UK. ISBN 1 55786 647 3

The three authors present a new paradigm on leadership. The focus is on personal mastery, group synergy and organisational learning.

Bennis Warren and Goldsmith Joan. *Learning To Lead* (1997). Nicholas Brealy, UK. ISBN 1 85788 198 2

The book differentiates between managing and leading and incorporate various exercises to promote awareness of leadership skills.

Berger Mel. *Cross-Cultural Team Building* (1996). The McGraw-Hill Publishing Co., UK. ISBN 0 07 707919 1

Berger, with the help of various contributors, combines theory and practice to highlight differences in culture and how these differences impact team-building in organisations.

Bleeke Joel and Ernst David. *Collaborating to Compete*
(1993). John Wiley, USA.                    ISBN 0 471 58009 0

The authors, who are from McKinsey & Co., provide guide to
designing effective cross-border alliances.

Brown Mark. *The Dinosaur Strain* (1993).
Innovation Centre Europe, UK.              ISBN 1 898379 00 9

Mark Brown pictures the activities in the dinosaur organisation
consisting of 'yes, but...' people. The book is a guide to innovation
and creativity.

Burke Gerard and Peppard Joe. *Examining Business Process
Re-Engineering* (1995). Kogan Page, UK.      ISBN 0 7494 1637 8

This book is a collection of articles written by distinguished
academics and examines the substantive aspects of Business Process
Re-Engineering.

*Business Action Pocketbooks*. A series of concise but comprehensive reference books. Each one contains sections describing
particular aspects of a topic in detail and checklists with useful tips.

The books in this series include:

*   *Building Your Business*
*   *Developing Yourself and Your Staff*
*   *Finance and Profitability*
*   *Sales and Marketing*
*   *Effective Business Communications*
*   *Managing Projects and Operations*

Published by Thorogood Ltd, UK.

Carnall Colin A. (Ed.) *Strategic Change* (1997).
Butterworth-Heinemann, Oxford, UK. ISBN 0 7506 1932 5

Colenso Michael. *High Performing Teams* (1997).
Butterworth-Heinemann, Oxford, UK. ISBN 0 7506 3354 9

'In Brief' book covering advice on how to build high performing teams. There are various checklists and summaries.

Carnall Colin A. (Ed) *Strategic Change* (1997)
Butterworth-Heinemann, Oxford, UK. ISBN 07506 1932 5

This is a management reader covering articles on managing strategic change, organisation change, strategic diagnosis, organisation transformation and programmes of change written by various experts including Charles Handy, Peter Senge, Chris Argyris, C.K. Prahalad and Y. L. Doz.

Covey Stephen R. *The Seven Habits of Highly Effective People* (1989). Simon & Schuster, USA. ISBN 0 671 71117 2

Much-acclaimed book dealing with solving personal and profess-ional problems. The focus of the book is on fairness, integrity, honesty and human dignity.

Crainer Stewart. *Key Management Ideas* (1990).
FT Pitman Publishing, UK. ISBN 0 273 62195 5

As the title suggests, Crainer deals with key ideas in management, ideas that have impact on the management world.

Daft Richard L. *Organisation Theory and Design* (1998).
South-Western Publishing, USA. ISBN 0 538 87902 5

A textbook covering all aspects of organisational design, systems and development.

De Wit Bob and Meyer Ron. *Strategy, Process, Content, Context* (1994). West Publishing Co., USA.  ISBN 0 314 03213 4

A substantive coverage of strategy with an international perspective.

de Bono Edward. *Teach Yourself To Think* (1996).
Penguin Books, UK.  ISBN 0 14 023077 7

The book very clearly explores different stages of thinking and directs us in putting thinking into action.

Drennan David. *Transforming Company Culture* (1992).
McGraw-Hill, UK.  ISBN 0 07 707660 5

This book uses many company examples to show step-by-step how to bring about change in your organisation.

Drucker Peter. *The Frontiers of Management* (1987).
Butterworth-Heinemann, Oxford, UK.  ISBN 04349 039 2

This book contains interviews and essays covering subjects under the headings of 'Economics Management' and 'The Organisation.' The topics explore challenges of tomorrow that face the executive today.

Evans Eric. *Mastering Negotiations* (1998).
Thorogood Ltd, UK.  ISBN 1 85418 195 5

Comprehensive coverage of different aspects of negotiation. The book adopts an action-centred approach to developing skills of negotiation.

Elkin Paul. *Mastering Business Planning and Strategy* (1998). Thorogood Ltd, UK.  ISBN 1 85418 190 4

The book covers the essential elements of Business Planning and Strategy.

Fritchie Rennie and Melling Magi. *The Business of Assertiveness* (1991). BBC, UK.     **ISBN 0 563 36196 4**

This book deals with basics of assertiveness, using assertiveness to handle conflicts and resolve problems.

Heresey Paul and Blanchard Ken. *Management of Organisational Behaviour* (1988). Prentice Hall, USA.     **ISBN 0 13 551433**

This is a standard textbook approach covering various human resources topics including Motivation, Leadership, Communications, Building Group Rapport and Relationships.

Hope Tony and Hope Jeremy. *Transforming the Bottom Line* (1995). Nicholas Brealey.     **ISBN 1 85788 102 8**

The book focuses on the quantitative aspect of organisational performance – 'Managing Performance with the Real Numbers.'

Kaplan Robert S and Norton David P. *The Balanced Scorecard* (1996). Harvard Business School Press, USA.

**ISBN 0 87584 651 3**

The authors are the architects of The Balanced Scorecard, the revolutionary tool to measure performance. The book covers financial perspective, customer perspective, internal-business-process perspective and learning and growth perspective.

Kay Maggie. *Who's the Boss Around Here, Anyway?* (1996). Rushmere Wynne, UK.     **ISBN 0 948035 39 0**

Many people experience stress overload. Maggie Kay deals with steps to regain control of our lives.

Kelly Terry. **Don't Put Socks on the Hippopotamus** (1998). Gower, UK. **ISBN** 0 566 07989 5

Terry Kelly covers in a very entertaining fashion, business rules relating to promotion, management, risk, change, communication and relationships.

Kermally Sultan. **Total Management Thinking** (1996) Butterworth-Heinemann, Oxford, UK. **ISBN** 0 7506 2614 3

This book covers key management ideas of the 1980s and 1990s. These ideas include the total quality management, benchmarking, customer service, business processing re-engineering, empowerment, delayering, teaming and knowledge era. Each chapter is supported by cases of organisations which have implemented these ideas and their experiences.

Kermally Sultan. **Managing Performance** (1997). Butterworth-Heinemann, Oxford, UK. **ISBN** 0 7506 3607 6

Various dimensions of performance measurement and management are covered here. It covers leadership, financial dimension, customer dimension , employees' dimension, corporate culture and economic performance.

Kotler Philip. **Marketing Management. Analysis, Planning, Implementation, and Control** (Eighth edition). Prentice-Hall International, USA. **ISBN** 0 13 098005 6

This is a comprehensive book on marketing management covering all aspects from analysis to implementation and control.

Kouzes James M and Posner Barry Z. *Credibility* (1993). Jossey-Bass Publishers, USA. ISBN 1 55542 550 X

This book is about leadership. The two authors identify the key to effective leadership. Their work is based on surveys of more than 15,000 people, 400 case studies and 40 in-depth interviews. Credibility emerges as a cornerstone of the effective leader.

Munro-faure Lesley, Munro-faure Malcolm, Bones Edward. *Achieving the New International Quality Standards* (1995). Pitman Publishing, UK. ISBN 0 27361977 2

Covers key aspects of ISO 9000, the framework for an effective quality management system, managing suppliers and controlling the production process.

Pascale Richard P. *Managing on the Edge* (1990). Penguin Book, UK. ISBN 0 14 014569 9

Pascale, with the aid of corporate cases, explains how to deal with conflict at work and how creating a positive conflict can lead to innovation.

Payne Adrian, Christopher Martin, Clark Moira and Peck Helen. *Relationship Marketing for Competitive Edge* (1995). Butterworth-Heinemann, Oxford, UK. ISBN 0 7506 2020

All four authors come from the Cranfield School of Management. The book brings together some of the best writing on the subject of Relationship Marketing. It covers issues relating to customer retention, employee satisfaction, supplier relations and management of service quality.

Peters Tom. *The Pursuit of WOW!* (1995).
Macmillan, UK. ISBN 0333 65084 0

A very provocative book on dealing with managing in a turbulent
times. The cover reads 'The Pursuit of WOW is a practical guide to
impractical times, containing the tactics and strategies you'll need
to get on the bullet trains.'

Peters Tom. *The Circle of Innovation* (1997).
Alfred A. Knope, USA. ISBN 0 375 40157 1

Another very provocative book in which Peters expresses, very
passionately, his views on innovation.

Pearson Barrie and Thomas Neil (Eds). *The Shorter MBA*
(1997) Thorogood, UK. ISBN 0 00 255830 0

This book covers Personal Development, Management Skills, and
Business Development.

Porter Michael, *Competitive Strategy* (1980).
The Free Press ISBN 002 0253 608

In this book, Porter presents various techniques for analysing
industries and competitors. It is a definitive work on the subject of
'competitive strategy.'

Sadler Peter. *Managing Talent* (1993). Century Business, UK.

ISBN 0 7126 9857 4

As the title suggests this book examines the concept of talent.
Recruitment and retention and how successful organisations deal
with talent to gain and sustain competitive advantage.

Savage Charles. *5th Generation Management* (1996).
Butterworth-Heinemann Oxford, UK.      **ISBN 0 7506 9701 6**

The book deals with the process of co-creation through virtual enterprising, dynamic teaming and knowledge networking.

Senge Peter. *The Fifth Discipline* (1990).
Century Business, UK.      **ISBN 0 7126 5687 1**

This book popularised the concept of 'the learning organisation'. It covers topics on Systems Thinking, Personal Mastery, Mental Models, Building Shared Vision and Team Learning.

Sherwood Dennis. *Unblock Your Mind* (1998). Gower, UK.

**ISBN 0 566 07983 6**

Sherwood covers the topic of innovation in a very lively and entertaining way.

Spencer John and Pruss Adrian. *How To Implement Change in your Company* (1993). Piatkus, UK.      **ISBN 0 7499 1258 8**

As the title suggests the coverage of the book deals with the drivers that affect change, preparing for change, making change happen and tools of change.

Spendolini Michael J. *The Benchmarking Book* (1992).
AMACOM, USA.      **ISBN 0 8144 7866 2**

The author explains the process of benchmarking and how to benchmark highlighting different stages of execution.

Thomas Neil (Ed). *The John Adair Handbook of Management and Leadership* (1998). Thorogood Ltd, UK.

This book covers key aspects of self management and managing others. It covers topics including time management, decision-making creativity, leadership, motivation and communication.

Thomas Mark. *Mastering People Management* (1998)
Thorogood Ltd, UK.                                    **ISBN 1 85418 096 7**

Thomas explains how to build and develop a successful team by motivating, empowering and leading people in organisations.

Tichy Noel M and Sherman Stratford. *Control Your Destiny or Someone Else Will* (1993). Harper Business, USA.

**ISBN 0 88730 670 5**

The book is presented as lessons in mastering change – the principles Jack Welch is using to revolutionise General Electric.

Vandermerwe Sandra. *From Tin Soldiers to Russian Dolls* (1993). Butterworth-Heinemann, Oxford, UK.    **ISBN 0 7506 0974 5**

The theme of the book is creating added value through services. The 'Russian Doll' creates the image of an interacting value chain incorporating customers as its focus.

Wickens Peter D. *The Ascendant Organisation* (1995).
Macmillan Business. UK.                               **ISBN 0 333 61130 6**

Wickens describes The Ascendant Organisation as 'an attempt to pull 'knowledge and 'know how' together'. This book is about people – their commitment and their leadership in an insecure environment. The author, who worked with Nissan in Sunderland brings in Japanese versus the West comparisons in relation to the idea of leadership and commitment.

Willcocks Graham and Morris Steve. *Putting Assertiveness to Work* (1996). Pitman Publishing, UK.    **ISBN 0 273 62331 1**

This book provides advice on how to recognise conflict and how to deal with various situations at work assertively.

Williams Allan, Dobson Paul, Walters Mike. *Changing Culture* (1989). Institute of Personnel Management, UK.

ISBN 0 85292 415 1

The book is based on a major research project. it explore the nature of corporate culture and examines various approaches to culture change.

# Useful articles

## Harvard Business Review

Henderson Rebecca. *Managing Innovation in the Information Age* January-February 1994. Pages 100-105.

Mintzberg Henry. *The Fall and Rise of Strategic Planning* January-February 1994. Pages 107-114.

Gouillart F and Sturdivant F. *Spend a Day in the Life of Your Customers* January-February 1994. Pages 116-125.

Bartlett Christopher and Goshal Sumantra. *Changing the Role of Top Management: Beyond Strategy to Purpose* November-December 1994. Pages 79-88.

McGahan Anita M. *Industry Structure and Competitive Advantage* November-December 1994. Pages 115-124.

Jones Thomas O and Sasser Jr. Earl W. *Why Satisfied Customers Defect* November-December 1995. Pages 88-99.

Prokesch Steven E. *Competing on Customer Service: An Interview with British Airways' Sir Colin Marshall* November-December 1995. Pages 100-116.

Kaplan Robert and Norton David. *Using the Balanced Scorecard as a Strategic Management System* January-February 1996. Pages 75-85.

Iacobucci Dawn. *The Quality Improvement Customers Didn't Want* January-February 1996. Pages 20-36.

Porter Michael. *What Is Strategy?* November-December 1996. Pages 61-78.

Teal Thomas. *The Human Side of Management* November-December 1996. Pages 35-44.

Heifetz Ronald A and Laurie Donald I. *The Work of Leadership* January-February 1997. Pages 124-134.

Pascale Richard, Millemann Mark and Gioja Linda. *Changing the Way we Change* November-December 1997. Pages 126-139.

Christensen Clayton M. *Making Strategy: Learning By Doing* November-December 1997. Pages 141-156.

Argyris Chris. *Empowerment: the Emperor's New Clothes* May-June 1998. Pages 98-105.

## European Management Journal

de Vries Manfred Kets. *Leaders Who Make Difference* No. 5. October 1996. Pages 486-493.

Smith Kenwyn and Berg David. *Cross-Cultural Groups at Work* No. 1. February 1997. Pages 8-15.

Angwin Duncan and Savill Brett. *Strategic Perspectives on European Cross-Border Acquisitions: A View From Top European Executives* No. 4. August 1997. Pages 423-435.

Clarke Angela and Grassed John. *Executive Briefing: Development of a Best Practice Model for a Change Management* No. 5, October 1997. Pages 537-545.

Cooper Robert. *Benchmarking New Product Performance: Results of the Best Practice Study* No. 1. February 1998. Pages 1-17.

Hiltropp Jean-Marie. *Preparing People for the Future: The Next Agenda for HRM* No.1. February 1998. Pages 70-78

Bruner Robert and Spekman Robert. *The Dark Side of Alliances: Lessons from Volvo Renault.* No.2. April 1998. Pages 136-150.

## Long Range Planning
## International Journal of Strategic Management

Hiltrop Jean M and Despres Charles. *Benchmarking the Performance of Human Resource Management* Issue 6. December 1994. Page 43.

Vandermerwe Sandra. *Becoming a Customer Owning a Corporation* Issue 6. December 1996. Page 770.

Lorange Peter. *Strategic Implementation* Issue 1. February 1998, Page 10

Kennedy Carol. *The Roadmap to Success: How Gerhard Schulmeyer Changed the Culture at Siemens Nixdorf* Issue 2. April 1998. Page 262.

Vaghefi Reza M and Huellmantel Alan B. *Strategic Leadership at General Electric* Issue 2. April 1998. Page 280.

Brouthers Keith D and van Hastenburg Paul and van der ven Joran. *If Most Mergers Fail Why Are They so Popular?* Issue 3. June 1998. Page 347.

Paper David. *BPR: Creating the Conditions for Success* Issue 3. June 1998. Page 426.

Newman Victor and Chaharbaghi Kazem. *The Corporate Culture Myth* Issue 4. August 1998. Page 514.

# Thorogood: the publishing business of the Hawksmere Group

**Thorogood publishes a wide range of books, reports, special briefings, psychometric tests and videos. Listed below is a selection of key titles.**

## Desktop Guides

The company director's desktop guide
*David Martin* • £15.99

The company secretary's desktop guide
*Roger Mason* • £15.99

The credit controller's desktop guide   *Roger Mason* • £15.99

The finance and accountancy desktop guide
*Ralph Tiffin* • £15.99

## Masters in Management

Mastering business planning and strategy
*Paul Elkin* • £19.99

Mastering financial management   *Stephen Brookson* • £19.99

Mastering leadership   *MichaelWilliams* • £19.99

Mastering negotiations   *Eric Evans* • £19.99

Mastering people management   *Mark Thomas* • £19.99

Mastering project management   *Cathy Lake* • £19.99

Mastering personal and interpersonal Skills
*Peter Haddon* • £16.99

## Essential Guides

The essential guide to buying and selling unquoted companies

*Ian Smith* • £25

The essential guide to business planning and raising finance

*Naomi Langford-Wood and Brian Salter* • £25

The essential business guide to the Internet

*Naomi Langford-Wood and Brian Salter* • £19.95

## Business Action Pocketbooks – *edited by David Irwin*

Building your business pocketbook                    £10.99

Developing yourself and your staff pocketbook        £10.99

Finance and profitability pocketbook                 £10.99

Managing and employing people pocketbook             £10.99

Sales and marketing pocketbook                       £10.99

## Other titles

The John Adair handbook of management and leadership

*Edited by Neil Thomas* • £19.95

The handbook of management fads          *Steve Morris* • £8.95

The inside track to successful management

*Dr Gerald Kushel* • £16.95

The pension trustee's handbook (2nd edition)

*Robin Ellison* • £25

Boost your company's profits          *Barrie Pearson* • £12.99

The art of headless chicken management

*Elly Brewer and Mark Edwards* • £6.99

EMU challenge and change – the implications for business

*John Atkin* • £11.99

Thorogood also has an extensive range of Reports and Special Briefings which are written specifically for professionals wanting expert information.

**For a full listing of all Thorogood publications, or to order any title, please call Thorogood Customer Services on 0171 824 8257 or fax on 0171 730 4293.**